Thomas Hughes

The manliness of Christ

Thomas Hughes

The manliness of Christ

ISBN/EAN: 9783337228057

Printed in Europe, USA, Canada, Australia, Japan

Cover: Foto ©ninafisch / pixelio.de

More available books at **www.hansebooks.com**

THE MANLINESS OF CHRIST.

BY

THOMAS HUGHES, Q. C.,
AUTHOR OF "TOM BROWN'S SCHOOL DAYS," ETC.

BOSTON:
HOUGHTON, OSGOOD AND COMPANY.
The Riverside Press, Cambridge.
1880.

NOTE.

THE greater part of the following pages appeared originally in "Good Words," and are now republished with the permission of the proprietors of that magazine.

T. H.

CONTENTS.

INTRODUCTORY.

	PAGE
THE MOTIVE OF THE BOOK	1

PART I.

THE HOLY LAND A. D. 30 — THE BATTLE FIELD OF THE GREAT CAPTAIN	8

PART II.

THE TESTS OF MANLINESS	17

PART III.

CHRIST'S BOYHOOD	35

PART IV.

THE CALL OF CHRIST	61

PART V.

CHRIST'S MINISTRY. ACT I.	77

CONTENTS.

PART VI.

	PAGE
CHRIST'S MINISTRY. ACT II.	95

PART VII.

CHRIST'S MINISTRY. ACT III. 110

PART VIII.

THE LAST ACT 126

CONCLUSION 137

THE MANLINESS OF CHRIST.

INTRODUCTORY.

THE MOTIVE OF THE BOOK.

Some time ago, when I was considering what method it would be best to adopt in Sunday-afternoon readings with a small class in the Working Men's College, I received a communication which helped me to come to a decision. It came in the form of a proposal for a new association, to be called "The Christian Guild." The promoters were persons living in our northern towns, some of which had lately gained a bad reputation for savage assaults and crimes of violence. My correspondents believed that some organized effort ought to be made to meet this evil, and that there was nothing in existence which would serve their purpose. The Young Men's Christian Associations had increased of late, indeed, in numbers, but had failed to reach the class which most needed Christian influences. There was a wide-spread feeling, they said, that these associations — valuable as they allowed them to be in many ways — did not cultivate individual manliness in their members, and that this defect was closely connected with their open profession of Christianity. They had separated their members too much from the ordinary habits and life of young men; and had set before them a wrong standard, which taught, not that they were to live in the world and subdue it to their Master, but were to withdraw from it as much as possible.

Therefore they would found their new "Christian Guild" on quite other principles. They aimed, indeed, at something like a revival of the muscular Christianity of twenty-five years ago, organized for missionary work in the great northern towns.

The members of the Guild must be first of all Christians, but selected as far as possible for some act of physical courage or prowess. It was proposed that the medal of the Royal Humane Society, or the championship of a town or district in running, wrestling, rowing, or other athletic exercise, should qualify at once for membership. These first members were to form the root, as it were, out of which branches of the Guild were to grow — one, they hoped, in every great centre of population. Each branch, if properly supported, might attract the most vigorous and energetic young men of its district, and so by degrees give a higher tone to the sports and occupations which absorb the spare time and energies of young Englishmen.

I did not see my way to joining any such movement, which, indeed, never seemed at all hopeful to me; nor do I know whether anything more has been done in the matter. But the proposal set me thinking on the state of things amongst us which the

Christian Guild was intended to meet. I was obliged to admit that my own experience, now stretching over a quarter of a century in London, agreed to some extent with that of my northern correspondents. Here, too, this same feeling exists, or it may be this same prejudice, as to "Young Men's Christian Associations" amongst the class from which their members are for the most part taken. Their tone and influence are said to lack manliness, and the want of manliness is attributed to their avowed profession of Christianity. If you pursue the inquiry, you will often come upon a distinct belief that this weakness is inherent in our English religion; that our Christianity does appeal and must appeal habitually and mainly to men's fears — to that in them which is timid and shrinking, rather than to that which is courageous and outspoken. This strange delusion is often alleged as the cause of the want of power and attraction in these associations.

I do not myself at all share this opinion

as to the Young Men's Christian Associations, for, so far as I have had the means of judging, they seem to me, especially in the last few years, to have been doing excellent service, though they work in a narrow groove. But whether this be so or not is a matter of comparative indifference, and the controversy may safely be left to settle itself. But the underlying belief in the rising generation that Christianity is really responsible for this supposed weakness in its disciples, is one which ought not to be so treated. The conscience of every man recognizes courage as the foundation of manliness, and manliness as the perfection of human character, and if Christianity runs counter to conscience in this matter, or indeed in any other, Christianity will go to the wall.

But does it? On the contrary, is not perfection of character — "Be ye perfect as your Father in heaven is perfect," perfection to be reached by moral effort in the faithful following of our Lord's life on earth — the final aim which the Christian religion sets before individual men; and constant contact and conflict with evil of all kinds the necessary condition of that moral effort, and the means adopted by our Master, in the world in which we live, and for which He died? In that strife, then, the first requisite is courage or manfulness, gained through conflict with evil, — for without such conflict there can be no perfection of character, the end for which Christ says we were sent into this world. But was Christ's own character perfect in this respect, — not only in charity, meekness, purity, long-suffering, but in courage? If not, can He be anything more than the highest and best of men, even if He were that; can He be the Son of God in any sense except that in which all men are sons?

This was the question which was forced on me at the time by the proposals of the Christian Guild, and it gave me the hint I was in search of as to the method of our

Sunday readings. We followed it up as well as we could through the events recorded in the gospels, applying the test at every stage of the drama. The results are collected in the following papers.

PART I.

THE HOLY LAND A. D. 30 — THE BATTLE FIELD OF THE GREAT CAPTAIN.

"Phœnicia and Palestine were sometimes annexed to and sometimes separated from the jurisdiction of Syria. The former was a narrow and rocky coast; the latter was a territory scarcely superior to Wales in fertility or extent! Yet Phœnicia and Palestine will ever live in the memory of mankind, since America as well as Europe has received letters from the one and religion from the other." — GIBBON, chap. i.

IN order to approach our subject with any chance of making the central figure clear to ourselves, and getting out of the atmosphere of unreality in which our ordinary religious training is too apt to leave us, we must make an effort to understand the condition and the surroundings of life in Palestine when our Lord appeared in it as a leader and teacher.

Take first the southern portion, the scene of the opening and closing days of His ministry, and of periodical visits during those three years. While He was still a boy under ten years of age the Romans had deposed Herod Archelaus, and had annexed Judæa, which was from thenceforth ruled as a province of the Empire by a Roman procurator. The rebellion of Judas of Gamala, which followed shortly afterwards, was a fierce protest of the Jews against the imperial taxation and the yoke of Rome. It was suppressed in the stern, Roman fashion, and from that time till the commencement of Christ's public ministry Jerusalem and the surrounding country were on the verge of revolt, a constant source of anxiety to the Roman procurators, and held down with difficulty by the heavy hand of the legions which garrisoned them.

All that was best and worst in the Jewish character and history combined to render the Roman yoke intolerably galling to the nation. The peculiar position of Jerusalem — a sort of Mecca to the tribes acknowledging the Mosaic law — made Syria the most dangerous of all the Roman provinces. To that city enormous crowds of pilgrims, of the most stiff-necked and fanatical of all races, flocked three times at least in every year, bringing with them offerings and tribute for the temple and its guardians, on a scale which must have made the hierarchy at Jerusalem formidable even to the world's master, by their mere command of wealth.

But this would be the least of the causes of anxiety to the Roman governor, as he spent year after year face to face with these terrible leaders of a terrible people.

These high priests and rulers of the Jews were indeed quite another kind of adversaries from the leaders, secular or religious, of any of those conquered countries which the Romans were wont to treat with contemptuous toleration. They still represented living traditions of the glory and sanctity of their nation, and of Jerusalem, and exercised still a power over that nation which the most resolute and ruthless of Roman procurators did not care wantonly to brave.

At the same time the yoke of high priest and scribe and pharisee was even heavier on the necks of their own people than that of the Roman. They had built up a huge superstructure of traditions and ceremonies round the law of Moses, which they held up to the people as more sacred and binding than the law itself. This superstructure was their special charge. This was, according to them, the great national inheritance, the most valuable portion of the covenant which God had made with their fathers. To them, as leaders of their nation, — a select, priestly, and learned caste, — this precious inheritance had been committed. Outside that caste, the dim multitude, "the people which knoweth not the law," were despised while they obeyed, accursed as soon as they showed any sign of disobedience. Such being the state of Judæa, it would not be easy to name in all history a less hopeful place for the reforming mission of a young carpenter, a stranger from a despised province, one entirely outside the ruling caste, though of the royal race, and who had no position whatever in any rabbinical school.

In Galilee the surroundings were slightly different, but scarcely more promising. Herod Antipas, the weakest of that tyrant family, the seducer of his brother's wife, the fawner on Cæsar, the spendthrift oppressor of the people of his tetrarchy, still ruled in name over the country, but with Roman garrisons in the cities and strongholds. Face to face with him, and exercising an *imperium in imperio* throughout Galilee, were the same priestly caste, though far less formidable to the civil power, and to the people, than in the southern province. Along the western coast of the Sea of Galilee, the chief scene of our Lord's northern ministry, lay a net-work of towns densely inhabited, and containing a large admixture of Gentile traders. This infusion of foreign blood, the want of any such religious centre as Jerusalem, and the contempt with which the southern Jews regarded their provincial brethren of Galilee, had no doubt loosened to some extent the yoke of the priests and scribes and lawyers in that province. But even here their traditionary power over the masses of the people was very great, and the consequences of defying their authority as penal, though the·penalty might be neither so swift or so certain, as in Jerusalem itself. Such was the society into which Christ came.

It is not easy to find a parallel case in the modern world, but perhaps the nearest exists in a portion of our own empire. The condition of parts of India in our day resembles in some respects that of Palestine in the year A. D. 30. In the Mahratta country, princes, not of the native dynasty, but the descendants of foreign courtiers (like the Idumæan Herods), are reigning. British residents at their courts, hated and feared, but practically all-powerful as Roman procurators, answer to the officers and garrisons of Rome in Palestine. The people are in bondage to a priestly caste scarcely less heavy than that which weighed on the Judæan and Galilean peasantry. If the Mahrattas were Mohammedans, and Mecca were situate in the territory of Scindiah or Holkar; if the influence of twelve centuries of Christian training could be wiped out of the English character, and the stubborn and fierce nature of the Jew substituted for that of the Mahratta; a village reformer amongst them, whose preaching outraged the Brahmins, threatened the dynasties, and disturbed the English residents, would start under somewhat similar conditions to those which surrounded Christ when He commenced his ministry.

In one respect, and one only, the time seemed propitious. The mind and heart of the nation was full of the expectation of a coming Messiah—a King who should break every yoke from off the necks of his people, and should rule over the nations, sitting on the throne of David. The intensity of this expectation had, in the opening days of his ministry, drawn crowds into the wilderness beyond Jordan from all parts of Judæa and Galilee, at the summons of a preacher who had caught up the last cadence of the song of their last great prophet, and was proclaiming that both the deliverance and the kingdom which they were looking for were at hand. In those crowds who flocked to hear John the Baptist there were doubtless some even amongst the priests and scribes, and many amongst the poor Jewish and Galilean peasantry, who felt that there was a heavier yoke upon them than that of Rome or of Herod Antipas. But the record of the next three years shows too clearly that even these were wholly unprepared for any other than a kingdom of this world, and a temporal throne to be set up in the holy city.

And so, from the first, Christ had to contend not only against the whole of the established powers of Palestine, but against the highest aspirations of the best of his countrymen. These very Messianic hopes, in fact, proved the greatest stumbling-block in his path. Those who entertained them most vividly had the greatest difficulty in accepting the carpenter's son as the promised Deliverer. A few days only before the end He had sorrowfully to warn the most intimate and loving of his companions and disciples, "Ye know not what spirit ye are of."

We must endeavor to keep these external conditions and surroundings of the life of a Galilean peasant in the reigns of Augustus and Tiberius Cæsar in our minds, if we really wish honestly to understand and appreciate the work done by one of them in those three short years, or the character of the doer of it.

PART II.

THE TESTS OF MANLINESS.

"Obvius in palatio Julius Atticus speculator, cruentum gladium ostentans, occisum a se Othonem, exclamavit; et Galba, 'Commilito,' inquit, 'quis jussit?' insigni animo ad coercendam militarem licentiam, minantibus intrepidus, adversus blandientes incorruptus." — *Tacit. Hist.*, lib. i., cap. xxxv.

ONE other precaution we must take at the outset of our inquiry, and that is, to settle for ourselves, without diverging into useless metaphysics, what we mean by "manliness, manfulness, courage." My friends of the Christian Guild seemed to assume that these words all have the same meaning, and denote the same qualities. Now, is this so? I think not, if we take the common use of the words. "Manliness and manfulness" are synonymous, but they embrace more than we ordinarily mean by the word "courage;" for instance, tenderness, and thoughtfulness for others. They include that courage which lies at the root of all manliness, but is, in fact, only its lowest or rudest form. Indeed, we must admit that it is not exclusively a human quality at all, but one which we share with other animals, and which some of them — for instance, the bulldog and weasel — exhibit with a certainty and a thoroughness which is very rare amongst mankind.

In what, then, does courage, in this ordinary sense of the word, consist? First, in persistency, or the determination to have one's own way, coupled with contempt for safety and ease, and readiness to risk pain or death in getting one's own way. This is, let us readily admit, a valuable, even a noble quality, but an animal quality rather than a human or manly one, and obviously not that quality of which the promoters of the Christian Guild were in search. For I fear we cannot deny that this kind of courage is by no means incompatible with those savage or brutal habits of violence which the Guild was specially designed to put down and root out amongst our people. What they desired to cultivate was obviously, not animal, but manly, courage; and the fact that we are driven to use these epithets "animal" and "manly" to make our meaning clear, shows, I think, the necessity of insisting on this distinction and keeping it well in mind.

We should note, also, that the tests of the Guild were, with one exception, not really adapted as tests even of animal courage, much less of manliness. For they proposed that the possession of the Royal Humane Society's medal, or the badge of excellence in athletic games, should be the qualification for the first members. Now the possession of the medal does amount to *primâ facie* evidence, not only of animal courage but of manliness; for it can only be won by an act involving not only persistency and contempt of pain and danger, but self-sacrifice for the welfare of another. But proficiency in athletic games has no such meaning, and is not necessarily a test even of animal courage, but only of muscular power and physical training. Even in those games which, to some extent, do afford a test of the persistency, and contempt for discomfort or pain, which constitute animal courage, — such as rowing, boxing, and wrestling, — it is of necessity a most unsatisfactory one. For instance, Nelson, — as courageous an Englishman as ever lived, who attacked a Polar bear with a handspike when he was a boy of fourteen, and told his captain, when he was scolded for it, that he did not know Mr. Fear, — with his slight frame and weak constitution, could never have won a boat race, and in a match would have been hopelessly astern of any one of the crew of his own barge; and the highest courage which ever animated a human body would not enable the owner of it, if he were himself untrained, to stand for five minutes against a trained wrestler or boxer.

Athleticism is a good thing if kept in its

place, but it has come to be very much over-praised and over-valued amongst us, as I think these proposals of the Christian Guild, for the attainment of their most admirable and needful aim, tend to show clearly enough, if proof were needed. We may say, then, I think, without doubt, that its promoters were not on the right scent, or likely to get what they were in search of by the methods they proposed to use. For after getting their Society of Athletes it might quite possibly turn out to be composed of persons deficient in real manliness.

While, however, keeping this conclusion well in mind, we need not at all depreciate athleticism, which has in it much that is useful to society, and is indeed admirable enough in its own way. But as the next step in our inquiry, let us bear well in mind that athleticism is not what we mean here. True manliness is as likely to be found in a weak as in a strong body. Other things being equal, we may perhaps admit (though I should hesitate to do so) that a man with a highly-trained and developed body will be more courageous than a weak man. But we must take this caution with us, that a great athlete may be a brute or a coward, while a truly manly man can be neither.

Having got thus far, and satisfied ourselves what is not of the essence of manliness, though often assumed to be so (as by the promoters of the Christian Guild), let us see if we cannot get on another step, and ascertain what is of that essence. And here it may be useful to take a few well-known instances of courageous deeds and examine them; because if we can find out any common quality in them we shall have lighted on something which is of the essence of, or inseparable from, that manliness which includes courage — that manliness of which we are in search.

I will take two or three at hazard from a book in which they abound, and which was a great favorite here some years ago, as I hope it is still, I mean Napier's "Peninsular War." At the end of the storming of Badajoz, after speaking of the officers, Napier goes on, "Who shall describe the springing valor of that Portuguese grenadier who was killed the foremost man at Santa Maria? or the martial fury of that desperate rifleman, who, in his resolution to win, thrust himself beneath the chained sword blades, and then suffered the enemy to dash his head in pieces with the ends of their muskets." Again, at the Coa, "a north of Ireland man named Stewart, but jocularly called 'the Boy,' because of his youth, nineteen, and of his gigantic stature and strength, who had fought bravely and displayed great intelligence beyond the river, was one of the last men who came down to the bridge, but he would not pass. Turning round he regarded the French with a grim look, and spoke aloud as follows: 'So this is the end of our brag. This is our first battle, and we retreat! The boy Stewart will not live to hear that said.' Then striding forward in his giant might he fell furiously on the nearest enemies with the bayonet, refused the quarter they seemed desirous of granting, and died fighting in the midst of them."

"Still more touching, more noble, more heroic, was the death of Sergeant Robert McQuade. During McLeod's rush this man, also from the north of Ireland, saw two men level their muskets on rests against a high gap in a bank, awaiting the uprise of an enemy. The present Adjutant-general Brown, then a lad of sixteen, attempted to ascend at the fatal spot. McQuade, himself only twenty-four years of age, pulled him back, saying, in a calm, decided tone, 'You are too young, sir, to be killed,' and then offering his own person to the fire fell dead pierced with both balls." And, speaking of the British soldier generally, he says in his preface, "What they were their successors now are. Witness the wreck of the Birkenhead, where four hundred men, at the call of their heroic officers, Captains Wright and Girardot, calmly and without a murmur accepted death in a horrible form rather than endanger the women and children saved in the boats. The records of the world furnish no parallel to this self-devotion." Let us add to these two very recent examples of which we have all been reading in the last few months: the poor colliers who worked day and night at Pont-y-pridd, with their lives in their hands, to rescue their buried comrades; and the gambler in St. Louis who went straight from the gaming-table into the fire, to the rescue of women and children, and died of the hurts after his third return from the flames.

Looking, then, at these several cases, we find in each that resolution in the actors to have their way, contempt for ease, and readiness to risk pain or death, which we noted as the special characteristics of animal courage, which we share with the bull-dog and weasel.

So far all of them are alike. Can we get any further? Not much, if we take the case of the rifleman who thrust his head under the sword-blades and allowed his brains to be knocked out sooner than draw it back, or that of "the boy Stewart." These are intense assertions of individual will and force,— avowals of the rough hard-handed man that he has that in him which enables him to defy pain and danger and death, — this and little or nothing more; and no doubt a very valuable and admirable thing as it stands.

But we feel, I think, at once, that there *is* something more in the act of Sergeant McQuade, and of the miners in Pont-y-pridd — something higher and more admirable. And it is not a mere question of degree, of more or less, in the quality of animal courage. The rifleman and "the boy Stewart" were each of them persistent to death, and no man can be more. The acts were, then, equally courageous, so far as persistency and scorn of danger and death are concerned. We must look elsewhere for the difference, for that which touches us more deeply in the case of Sergeant McQuade than in that of "the boy Stewart," and can only find it in the motive. At least it seems to me that the worth of the last lies mainly in the sublimity of self-assertion, of the other in the sublimity of self-sacrifice.

And this holds good again in the case of the Birkenhead. Captain Wright gave the word for the men to fall in on deck by companies, knowing that the sea below them was full of sharks, and that the ship could not possibly float till the boats came back; and the men fell in, knowing this also, and stood at attention without uttering a word, till she heeled over and went down under them. And Napier, with all his delight in physical force and prowess, and his intense appreciation of the qualities which shine most brightly in the fiery action of battle, gives the palm to these when he writes, " The records of the world furnish no parallel to this self-devotion." He was no mean judge in such a case; and, if he is right, as I think he is, do we not get another side-light on our inquiry, and find that the highest temper of physical courage is not to be found, or perfected, in action but in repose? All physical effort relieves the strain, and makes it easier to persist unto death, under the stimulus and excitement of the shock of battle, or of violent exertion of any kind, than when the effort has to be made with grounded arms. In other words, may we not say that in the face of danger self-restraint is after all the highest form of self-assertion, and a characteristic of manliness as distinguished from courage?

But we have only been looking hitherto at one small side of a great subject, at the courage which is tested in times of terror, on the battle-field, in the sinking ship, the poisoned mine, the blazing house. Such testing times come to few, and to these not often in their lives. But, on the other hand, the daily life of every one of us teems with occasions which will try the temper of our courage as searchingly, though not as terribly, as battle-field or fire or wreck. For we are born into a state of war; with falsehood and disease and wrong and misery, in a thousand forms, lying all around us, and the voice within calling on us to take our stand as men in the eternal battle against these.

And in this life-long fight, to be waged by every one of us single-handed against a host of foes, the last requisite for a good fight, the last proof and test of our courage and manfulness, must be loyalty to truth — the most rare and difficult of all human qualities. For such loyalty, as it grows in perfection, asks ever more and more of us, and sets before us a standard of manliness always rising higher and higher.

And this is the great lesson which we shall learn from Christ's life, the more earnestly and faithfully we study it. "For this end was I born, and for this cause came I into the world, to bear witness to the truth." To bear this witness against avowed and open enemies is comparatively easy. But to bear it against those we love, against those whose judgment and opinions we respect, in defense or futherance of that which approves itself as true to our own inmost conscience, this is the last and abiding test of courage and of manliness. How natural, nay, how inevitable it is, that we should fall into the habit of appreciating and judging things mainly by the standards in common use amongst those we respect and love. But these very standards are apt to break down with us when we are brought face to face with some question which takes us ever so little out of ourselves and our usual moods. At such times we are driven to admit in our hearts that we, and those we respect and love, have been looking at and judging things, not truthfully, and therefore not courageously and manfully, but conventionally. And then comes one of the most searching of all trials of courage and manliness, when a man or woman is called to stand by what approves itself to their consciences as true, and to protest for it through evil report and good report, against all discouragement and opposition from those they love or respect. The sense of antagonism instead of rest, of distrust and alienation instead of approval and sympathy, which such times bring, is a test which tries the very heart and reins, and it is one which meets us at all ages, and in all conditions of life. Emerson's hero is the man who, "taking both reputation and life in his hand, will with perfect urbanity dare the gibbet and the mob, by the absolute truth of his speech and rectitude of his behavior." And, even in our peaceful and prosperous England, absolute truth of speech and rectitude of behavior will not fail to bring their fiery trials, if also in the end their exceeding great rewards.

We may note, too, that in testing manliness as distinguished from courage, we shall have to reckon sooner or later with the idea of duty. Nelson's column stands in the most conspicuous site in all London, and stands there with all men's approval, not because of his daring courage. Lord Peterborough in a former generation, Lord Dundonald in the one which succeeded, were at least as eminent for reckless and successful daring. But it is because the idea of devotion to duty is inseparably connected with Nelson's name in the minds of Englishmen, that he has been lifted high above all his compeers in England's capital.

In the throes of one of the terrible revolutions of the worst days of imperial Rome, — when probably the cruellest mob and most licentious soldiery of all time were raging round the palace of the Cæsars, and the chances of an hour would decide whether Galba or Otho should rule the world, the alternative being a violent death, — an officer of the guard, one Julius Atticus, rushed into Galba's presence with a bloody sword, boasting that he had slain his rival, Otho. "My comrade, by whose order?" was his only greeting from the old Pagan chief. And the story has come down through eighteen centuries, in the terse strong sentences of the great historian prefixed to this chapter, a test for all times.

Comrade, who ordered thee? whose will art thou doing? It is the question which has to be asked of every fighting man, in whatever part of the great battle-field he comes to the front, and determines the manliness of soldier, statesman, parson, of every strong man, and suffering woman.

> "Three roots bear up Dominion : knowledge, will,
>   These two are strong ; but stronger still the third,
>   Obedience : 'tis the great tap root, which still,
>   Knit round the rock of Duty, is not stirred,
> Though storm and tempest spend their utmost skill."

I think that the more thoroughly we sift and search out this question the more surely we shall come to this as the conclusion of the whole matter. Tenacity of will, or wilfulness, lies at the root of all courage, but courage can only rise into true manliness when the will is surrendered; and the more absolute the surrender of the will the more perfect will be the temper of our courage and the strength of our manliness.

> "Strong Son of God, immortal Love,"

our laureate has pleaded, in the moment of his highest inspiration,

> "Our wills are ours to make them thine."

And that strong Son of God to whom this cry has gone up in our day, and in all days, has left us the secret of his strength in the words, "I am come to do the will of my Father and your Father."

PART III.

CHRIST'S BOYHOOD.

> "So close is glory to our dust,
> So near is God to man;
> When duty whispers low, Thou must,
> The youth replies, I can." — EMERSON.

ONE great difficulty meets the student of our Lord's life and character from whatever side, and with whatever purpose, he may approach it. The whole authentic record of that life, up to the time of his baptism, when He was already thirty years old, is comprised in half-a-dozen sentences. All that we know is the story of his visit to Jerusalem at the age of twelve, when He was lost in the crush of the great feast, and his parents turned back to look for Him: "And it came to pass, that after three days they found Him in the temple, sitting at the feet of the doctors, both hearing them and asking them questions. And all that heard

Him were astonished at his understanding and answers. And when they saw Him they were amazed, and his mother said unto Him, Son, why hast thou so dealt with us? Behold, thy father and I have sought thee sorrowing. And He said unto them, How is it that ye sought me? Wist ye not that I must be about my Father's business? And they understood not this saying which He spake unto them. And He went down to Nazareth and was subject unto them."

The silence of the evangelists as to all other details of his youth and early manhood, except this one short incident, which belongs rather to his public than to his private life, is intended no doubt to fix our attention on the former, as that which most concerns us. At the same time it is impossible for those who will follow, as best they may, Christ's steps and teaching, setting before themselves that highest outcome and aim of it all, " be ye perfect as your Father in heaven is perfect," not to turn often in thought to those early years of his in which the weapons must have been forged, and the character formed and matured, for the mighty war.

And it cannot be denied that, to such seekers, this short temple story is in many ways baffling, even discouraging. There is something at first sight, willful indeed, possibly courageous, but not manly, in a boy of twelve staying behind his parents in a strange city without their knowledge or consent; something thoughtless, almost ungracious, in the words of reply to Mary's "thy father and I have sought thee sorrowing" — "How is it that ye sought me? wist ye not that I must be about my Father's business?" (or "in my Father's courts," as the words are more truly translated).

The clue to this apparent divergence from the perfect manly life is given with rare insight and beauty in Mr. Holman Hunt's great picture. At any rate the face and attitude of the boy there seemed for the first time to make clear to me the meaning of the recorded incident, and to cast a flood of light on those eighteen years of preparation which yet remained before He should be ready for his public work. The real meaning and scope of that work, in all its terrible majesty and suffering and grandeur, have just begun to dawn on the boy's mind. The first sight of Jerusalem, and of the temple, has stirred new and strange thoughts within Him. The replies of the doctors to his eager questionings have lighted up the consciousness which must have been dimly working in Him already, that he was not altogether like those around Him — the children with whom He was accustomed to play, the parents at whose knees He had been brought up.

Many of us must have seen, all must have read of, instances of a call to their spirits being clearly recognized by very young children, and coloring and molding their whole after lives. We can scarcely say how early this awakening of a consciousness of what he is, of what he is meant to do, has come to this or that young child, but no one will question that it does so come in many instances long before the age of twelve. And so I think we may safely assume that when Christ came up for the first time to the feast which commemorated the great deliverance of his nation, the boy was already conscious of a voice within, calling Him to devote Himself to the work to which the God of his fathers had in like manner called in their turn, Moses, and Samuel, and David, and Elijah, and Judas Maccabæus, and all that grand roll of patriot prophets, and kings, and warriors, with whose names and doings He would be already familiar. Amidst all the pomp of the great festival He found the chosen people weighed down by a sterner and more degrading bondage than had befallen them in all their long annals. And all that He heard and saw in the holy city, amongst the crowds of worshippers, and the rabbis teaching in the temple courts —

the first view of the holy hill of Sion, the joy of the whole earth — the strange contrast of the eager traffic, the gross Mammon worship, the huge slaughtering of beasts with all the brutal accompaniments, with that universal longing and expectation in those multitudes for the Messiah, who should lead and work out the final deliverance and triumph of the people of God in that generation — must have stirred new questionings within Him, questionings whether that voice which He had been already hearing in his own heart was not only *a* call, such as might come to any Hebrew boy, but *the* call — whether amongst all that vast assembly He was not the one upon whom the supreme task must be laid, who must be the deliverer of this people, so certainly and eagerly looked for.

To the young spirit before whose inward eye such a vision is opening all human ties would shrink back, and be for the moment forgotten. And, when recalled suddenly by the words of his mother, the half conscious dreamy answer, " How is it that ye sought me ? Wist ye not that I must be in my Father's courts, about his business ? " loses all its apparent willfulness and abruptness.

And so, full of this new question and great wonder, He went home to the village in Galilee with his parents, and was subject to them ; and the curtain falls for us on his boyhood and youth and early manhood. But as nothing but what is most important, and necessary for understanding all of his life which we need for our own growth into his likeness, is told in these simple gospel narratives, it would seem that this vivid light is thrown on that first visit to Jerusalem because it was the crisis in our Lord's early life which bears most directly on his work for our race. If so, we must, I think, allow that the question once fairly presented to the boy's mind would never again have left it. Day by day it would have been coming back with increasing insistency, gathering power and weight. And as He submitted it day by day to the God whom prophet and Psalmist had taught every child of the nation to look upon as " about his path and about his bed, and knowing every thought of his heart," the consciousness must have gained strength and power. As the habit of self-surrender and simple obedience to the voice within grew more perfect, and more a part of his very being, the call must have sounded more and more clearly.

And, as He was in all things tempted like as we are, again and again must his human nature have shrunk back and tried every way of escape from this task, the call to which was haunting Him; while every succeeding month and year of life must have disclosed to Him more and more of its peril and its hopelessness, as well as of its majesty.

We have, then, to picture to ourselves this struggle and discipline going on for eighteen years — the call sounding continually in his ears, and the boy, the youth, the strong man, each in turn solicited by the special temptations of his age, and rising clear above them through the strength of perfect obedience, the strength which comes from the daily fulfillment of daily duties — that "strength in the Lord" which St. Paul holds up to us as possible for every human being. Think over this long probation, and satisfy yourselves whether it is easy, whether it is possible to form any higher ideal of perfect manliness.

And without any morbid curiosity, and I think with profit, we may follow out the thoughts which this long period of quiet suggests. We know from the evangelists only this, that He remained in obscurity in a retired village of Galilee, and subject to his reputed father and mother. That He also remained in great seclusion while living the simple peasant life of Nazareth we may infer from the surprise, not unmixed with anger and alarm, of his own family, when, after his baptism, He began his public career amongst them. And yet, on that day when He rose to speak in the synagogue, it is clear that the act was one which commended itself in the first instance to his family and neighbors. The eyes of all present were at once fixed on Him as on one who might be expected to stand in the scribe's place, from whom they might learn something, a Man who had a right to speak.

Indeed, it is impossible to suppose that He could have lived in their midst from childhood to full manhood without attracting the attention, and stirring many questionings in the minds, of all those with whom He was brought into contact. The stories in the Apocryphal Gospels of the exercise of miraculous powers by Christ as a child and boy may be wholly disregarded; but we may be sure that such a life as his, though lived in the utmost possible seclusion, must have impressed every one with whom He came in contact, from the scribe who taught the Scriptures in Nazareth to the children who sat by his side to learn, or met Him by chance in the vineyards or on the hill-sides. That He was diligent in using such means for study as were within his reach, if it needed proof, would appear from his perfect familiarity with the laws and history of his country at the opening of his ministry. And the mysterious story of the crisis immediately following his baptism, in which He wrestled, as it were, face to face with the tempter and betrayer of mankind, indicates to us the nature of the daily battle which He must have been waging, from his earliest infancy, or at any rate ever since his first visit to Jerusalem. No one can suppose for a moment that the trial came on Him for the first time after the great prophet to whom all the nation were flocking had owned Him as the coming Christ. That recognition removed, indeed, the last doubt from his mind, and gave Him the signal for which He had been patiently waiting, that the time was come and He must set forth from his retirement. But the assurance that the call would come at some time must have been growing on Him in all those years, and so when it does come He is perfectly prepared.

In his first public discourse in the synagogue of Nazareth we find Him at once announcing the fulfillment of the hopes which all around Him were cherishing. He proclaims, without any preface or hesitation, with the most perfect directness and confidence, the full gospel of the kingdom of heaven. "The time is fulfilled, and the kingdom of God is at hand." He takes for the text of his first discourse the passage in Isaiah: "The Spirit of the Lord is upon me, because he hath anointed me to preach the gospel to the poor; he hath sent me to heal the broken-hearted, to preach deliverance to the captive, the recovery of sight to the blind, to set at liberty them that are bruised, to preach the acceptable year of the Lord," and proceeds to expound how "this day is this scripture fulfilled in your ears." And within the next few days He delivers his Sermon on the Mount, of which we have the full record, and in which we find the meaning, and character, and principles of the kingdom, laid down once and for all. Mark, that there is no hesitation, no ambiguity, no doubt as to who He is, or what message He has to deliver. "I have not come to destroy, but to fulfill the law which my Father and your Father has given you, and which you have misunderstood. This which I am now unfolding to you is the meaning of that law, this is the will of my Father who is in heaven."

Thus He springs at once, as it were, full-armed into the arena; and it is this thorough mastery of his own meaning and position from the first — this thorough insight into what He has to do, and the means by which it is to be done — upon which we should fix our thoughts if we want to understand, or to get any notion at all of, what must have been the training of those eighteen years.

How had this perfect insight and confidence been reached? "This young peasant, preaching from a boat or on a hill-side, sweeps aside at once the traditions of our most learned doctors, telling us that this, which we and our fathers have been taught, is not what the God of Israel intended in these commandments of his; but that He, this young Man, can tell us what God did really intend. He assumes to speak to us as one having authority. Who gave Him this authority?" These, we know, are the kind of questionings with which Christ was met at once, and over and over again. And they are most natural and necessary questionings, and must have occurred to Himself again and again, and been answered by Him to Himself, before He could have stood up to proclaim with the tone of absolute authority his good news to the village congregations in Galilee, or the crowds on the Mount, or by the lake.

Who gave thee this authority? We can only reverentially, and at a distance, picture to ourselves the discipline and struggles by which the answer was reached, which enabled Him to go out without the slightest faltering or misgiving, and deliver his full and astounding message, the moment the sign came that the time had come, and that it was indeed He to whom the task was entrusted.

But the lines of that discipline, which in a measure is also the discipline of every one of us, are clearly enough indicated for us in the story of the temptation.

In every subtle form this question must have been meeting the maturing Christ day after day. Art thou indeed the Son of God who is said to be coming to redeem this enslaved and degraded people, and with and beside them all the kingdoms of the world? Even if these prophets have not been dreaming and doting, art not Thou at least dreaming and doting? At any rate if that is your claim put it to some test. Satisfy yourself, and show us, while satisfying yourself, some proof of your title which we, too, can recognize. Here are all these material, visible things which, if your claim be true, must be subject to you. Show us your power over some of them — the meanest if you will, the common food which keeps men alive. There are spiritual invisible forces too, which are supposed to be the ministers of God, and should therefore be under the control of his Son — give us some sign that you can guide or govern the least of them. Why pause or delay? Is the burden growing lighter on this people? Is the Roman getting year by year less insolent, the publican less fraudulent and exacting, the Pharisees and rulers less godless, the people, your own kin amongst them, less degraded and less brutal? You are a grown man, with the full powers of a man at any rate. Why are you idling here when your Father's work (if God be your Father) lies broadcast on every side, and no man standing forth to " the help of the Lord against the mighty," as our old seers used to rave?

I hope I may have been able to indicate to you, however imperfectly, the line of thought which will enable each of you for yourselves to follow out and realize, more or less, the power and manliness of the character of Christ implied in this patient waiting in obscurity and doubt through the years when most men are at full stretch, — waiting for the call which shall convince Him that the voice within has not been a lying voice, — and meantime making Himself all that God meant Him to be, without haste and without misgiving.

In the time of preparation for the battle of life this is the true touchstone. Haste and distrust are the sure signs of weakness, if not of cowardice. Just in so far as they prevail in any life, even in the most heroic, the man fails, and his work will have to be done over again. In Christ's life up to the age of thirty there is not the slightest trace of such weakness, or cowardice. From all that we are told, and from all we can infer, He made no haste, and gave way to no doubt, waiting for God's mind, and patiently preparing Himself for whatever his work might be. And so his work from the first was perfect, and through his whole public life He never faltered or wavered, never had to withdraw or modify a word once spoken. And thus He stands, and will stand to the end of time, the true model of the courage and manliness of boyhood and youth and early manhood.

Before passing on to the public life of Christ, there is one point which has been raised, and upon which perhaps a few words should be said, although it does not directly bear upon our inquiry. I refer to the supernatural power which all Christians hold to have dwelt in Him, and to have been freely exercised within certain limits during his public career. Was He always conscious of it? And, if so, did He exercise it before his call and baptism? Here we get not the slightest direct help from the gospel narratives, and (as has been already said) no reliance whatever can be placed on the apocryphal stories of his boyhood. We are therefore left to our own judgment and reason, and there must always be differences between the conclusions at which one man and another will arrive, however honestly each may search for the truth.

To me, however, one or two matters seem to be clear enough. The first is, that He had only the same means as the rest of us of becoming conscious of his relationship to God. For, if this were not so, He is no example for us, He was not " tempted like as we are." Now the great difference between one man and another depends upon how these means are used; and, so far as they are used according to the mind and will of God, we gain mastery over ourselves and our surroundings. " As the world was plastic and fluid in the hands of God, so it is ever to so much of his attributes as we bring to it," may be a startling saying of Mr. Emerson's, but is one which commends itself to our experience and reason, if we only consult them honestly. Let us take the most obvious example of this law. Look at the relations of man to the brute creation. One of us shall have no difficulty in making friends of beasts and birds, while another excites their dread and hate, so that even dogs will scarcely come near him. There is no need to go back to the traditions of the hermits in the Thebaid, or St. Francis of Assisi, for instances of the former class. We all know the story of Cowper and his three hares from his exquisite letters and poem, and most of you must have read, or heard of the terms on which Waterton lived with the birds and beasts in his Yorkshire home, and of Thoreau, unable to get rid of wild squirrels and birds who would come and live with him, or from a boat taking up fish, which lay quietly in his hand till he chose to put them back again into the stream. But I suppose there is scarcely one of us who has not himself seen such instances again and again, persons of whom the old words seemed literally true, " At destruction and famine thou shalt laugh; neither shalt thou be afraid of the beasts of the earth. For thou shalt be in league with the stones of the field, and the beasts of the field shall be at peace with thee."

I remember myself several such; a boy who was friends even with rats, stoats, and snakes, and generally had one or other of them in his pockets; a groom upon whose shoulders the pigeons used to settle, and nestle against his cheeks, whenever he went out into the stable-yard or field. Is there any reasonable way of accounting for this? Only one, I think, which is, that those who have this power over, and attraction for, animals, have always felt towards them and treated them as their Maker intended — have unconsciously, perhaps, but still faithfully, followed God's mind in their dealings with his creatures, and so have stood in true relations to them all, and have found the beasts of the field at peace with them.

In the same way the stones of the field are in league with the geologist, the trees and flowers with the botanist, the component parts of earth and air with the chemist, just in so far as each, consciously or unconsciously, follows God's methods with them — each part of his creation yielding up its secrets and its treasures to the open mind of the humble and patient, who is also at bottom always the most courageous, learner.

And what is true of each of us beyond all question — what every man who walks with open eyes, and open heart, knows to be true of himself — must be true also of Christ. And so, though we may reject the stories of the clay birds, which He modeled as a child, taking wing and bursting into song round Him (as on a par with St. Francis's address to his sisters the swallows at Alvia, or the flocks in the Marches of Venice, who thereupon kept silence from their twitterings and songs till his sermon was finished), we cannot doubt that in proportion as Christ was more perfectly in sympathy with God's creation than any mediæval saint, or modern naturalist, or man of science, He had more power than they with all created things from his earliest youth. Nor could it be otherwise with the hearts and wills of men. Over these we know that, from that time to this, He has exercised a supreme sway, infinitely more wonderful than that over birds and beasts, because of man's power of resistance to the will Christ came to teach and to do, which exists, so far as we can see, in no other part of creation.

I think, then, it is impossible to resist the conclusion that He must have had all these powers from his childhood, that they must have been growing stronger from day to day, and He, at the same time, more and more conscious of possessing them, not to use on any impulse of curiosity or self-will, but only as the voice within prompted. And it seems the most convincing testimony to his perfect sonship, manifested in perfect obedience, that He should never have tested his powers during those thirty years as He did at once and with perfect confidence as soon as the call came. Had He done so his ministry must have commenced sooner; that is to say, before the method was matured by which He was to reconstruct, and lift into a new atmosphere and on to a higher plane, the faith and life of his own nation and of the whole world. For it is impossible to suppose that the works which He did, and the words He spoke, at thirty — which at once threw all Galilee and Judæa into a ferment of hope and joy and doubt and anger — should have passed unnoticed had they been wrought and spoken when He was twenty. Here, as in all else, He waited for God's mind: and so, when the time for action came, worked with the power of God. And this waiting and preparation must have been the supreme trial of his faith. The holding this position must have been in those early years the holding of the very centre of the citadel of Man's soul (as Bunyan so quaintly terms it), against which the assaults of the tempter must have been delivered again and again while the garrison was in training for the victorious march out into the open field of the great world, carrying forth the standard which shall never go back.

And while it may be readily admitted that Christ wielded a dominion over all created things, as well as over man, which no other human being has ever approached, it seems to me to be going quite beyond what can be proved, or even fairly assumed, to speak of his miracles as supernatural, in the sense that no man has ever done, or can ever do, the like. The evidence is surely all the other way, and seems rather to indicate that if we could only have lived up to the standard which we acknowledge in our inmost hearts to be the true one, — could only have obeyed every motion and warning of the voice of God speaking in our hearts from the day when we first became conscious of and could hear it, — if, in other words, our wills had from the first been disciplined, like the will of Christ, so as to be in perfect accord with the will of God, — I see no reason to doubt that we, too, should have gained the power and the courage to show signs, or, if you please, to work miracles, as Christ and his Apostles worked them.

PART IV.

THE CALL OF CHRIST.

"Sound, thou trumpet of God! come forth, great cause, to array us!
King and leader, appear! thy soldiers sorrowing seek thee."
A. CLOUGH.

AT last the good news for which they had been longing comes to the expecting nation. A voice is heard in the lonely tracts beyond Jordan — the route along which the caravans of pilgrims from Galilee passed so often, to and from the feasts at Jerusalem — proclaiming that the kingdom of heaven is at hand. The news is soon carried to the capital, and from Jerusalem and all Judæa, and all the region round about Jordan, the people go out to hear it; and, when they have heard it, are baptized in crowds, eagerly claiming each for himself a place in this kingdom. It gathers strength till it moves rulers and priests, council and Sanhedrim, as well as the people who know not the law; and presently priests and Levites are sent out from Jerusalem to test messenger and message, and ask, " Who art thou? What kingdom is this thou art proclaiming without our sanction?" It spreads northward also, and the despised Galileans from lake shore and half pagan cities flock down to hear it for themselves, and the simplest and bravest souls amongst them, such as Andrew and Simon Peter, to attach themselves to the preacher. From the highways and lake cities it pierces the Galilean valleys, and comes to the ears of Jesus, in the carpenter's cottage at Nazareth.

He, too, is moved by the call, and starts for the Jordan, filled, we may be sure, with the hope that the time for action has come at last, that the God of Israel is again about to send deliverance to his people. May we not also fairly conjecture that, on his way to Bethabara, to claim his place in the national confession and uprising, He must have had moments of rejoicing that the chief part in the great drama seemed likely after all to be laid on another? As a rule, the more thoroughly disciplined and fit a man may be for any really great work, the more conscious will he be of his own unfitness for it, the more distrustful of himself, the more anxious not to thrust himself forward. It is only the zeal of the half-instructed when the hour of a great deliverance has come at last — of those who have had a glimpse of the glory of the goal, but have never known or counted the perils of the path which leads to it — which is ready with the prompt response, "Yes — we can drink of the cup; we can be baptized with the baptism."

But in Christ, after the discipline of those long waiting years, there was no ambition, no self-delusion. He had measured the way, and counted the cost, of lifting his own people and the world out of bondage to visible things and false gods, and bringing them to the only Father of their spirits, into the true kingdom of their God. He must, indeed, have been well enough aware how infinitely more fit for the task He Himself was than any of his own brethren in the flesh, with whom He was living day by day, or of the men of Nazareth with whom He had been brought up. But He knew also that the same voice which had been speaking to him, the same wisdom which had been training him, must have been speaking to and training other humble and brave souls, wherever there were open hearts and ears, in the whole Jewish nation. As the humblest and most guileless of men He could not have assumed that no other Israelite had been able to render that perfect obedience of which He was Himself conscious. And so He may well have hurried to the Jordan in the hope of finding there, in this prophet of the wilderness, " Him who should come," the Messiah, the great deliverer — and of enlisting under his banner, and rendering Him true and loyal service, in the belief that, after all, He

Himself might only be intended to aid, and hold up the hands of a greater than Himself. For, we must remember that Christ could not have heard before He came to Bethabara that John had disclaimed the great title. It was not till the very day before his own arrival that the Baptist had told the questioners from Jerusalem, "I am not He."

But if any such thought had crossed his mind, or hope filled his heart, on the way to the Baptist, it was soon dispelled, and He, left again in his own loneliness, now more clearly than ever before, face to face with the task, before which even the Son of God, appointed to it before the world was, might well quail, as it confronted Him in his frail human body. For John recognizes Him, singles Him out at once, proclaims to the bystanders, " This is He! Behold the Lamb of God! This is He who shall baptize with the fire of God's own Spirit. Here is the deliverer whom all our prophets have foretold. And by a mysterious outward sign, as well as by the witness in his own heart and conscience, Christ is at once assured of the truth of the Baptist's words — that it is indeed He Himself and no other, and that his time has surely come.

That He now thoroughly realized the fact for the first time, and was startled and severely tried by the confirmation of what He must have felt for years to be probable, is not only what we should look for from our own experiences, but seems the true inference from the gospel narratives. For, although as soon as the full truth breaks upon Him He accepts the mission and work to which God is calling Him, and speaks with authority to the Baptist, " Suffer it to be so now," yet the immediate effect of the call is to drive Him away into the wilderness, there in the deepest solitude to think over once again, and for the last time to wrestle with and master, the tremendous disclosure. And the story of the temptation which immediately follows — so full of mystery and difficulty in many ways — is invaluable for the light which it casts, not only on this crisis of his life, but before and after — on the history of the world's redemption, and the method by which that redemption is to be accomplished, the part which each individual man and woman is called to play in it.

For Christ's whole life on earth was the assertion and example of true manliness — the setting forth in living act and word what man is meant to be, and how he should carry himself in this world of God's, — one long campaign, in which " the temptation " stands out as the first great battle and victory. The story has depths in it which we can never fathom, but also clear, sharp lessons which he who runs may read, and no man can master too thoroughly. We must follow Him reverently into the wilderness, where He flies from the crowds who are pressing to the Baptist, and who to-morrow will be thronging around Him, if He goes back amongst them, after what the Baptist has said about Him to-day.

Day after day in the wilderness the struggle goes on in his heart. He is faint from insufficient food in those solitudes, and with bodily weakness the doubts grow in strength and persistence, and the tempter is always at his side, soliciting Him to end them once for all, by one act of self-assertion. All those questionings and misgivings as to his origin and mission which we have pictured to ourselves as haunting Him ever since his first visit to Jerusalem, are now, as it were, focussed. There are mocking voices whispering again as of old, but more scornfully and keenly, in his ear, " Are you really the Messiah, the Son of God, so long looked for? What more proof have you to go upon than you have had for these many years, during which you have been living as a poor peasant in a Galilean village? The word of this wild man of the wilderness? He is your own cousin, and a powerful preacher, no doubt, but a wayward, willful man, clad and fed like a madman, who has been nursing mad fancies from his boyhood, away from the holy city, the centre of national life and learning. This sign of a descending dove, and a voice which no one has heard but yourself? Such signs come to many, — are never wanting when men are ready to deceive themselves, — and each man's fancy gives them a different meaning. But the words, and the sign, and the voice, you say, only meet a conviction which has been growing these thirty years in your own heart and conscience? Well, then, at least for the sake of others if not for your own sake, put this conviction to the proof, here, at once, and make sure yourself, before you go forth and deceive poor men, your brethren, to their ruin. You are famishing here in the wilderness. ·This, at least, cannot be what God intends for his Son, who is to redeem the world. Exercise some control over the meanest part of your Father's kingdom. Command these stones to become bread, and see whether they will obey you. Cast yourself down from this height. If you are what you think, your

Father's angels will bear you up. Then, after they have borne you up, you may go on with some reasonable assurance that your claim is not a mere delusion, and that you will not be leading these poor men whom you call your brethren to misery and destruction."

And when neither long fasting and weakness, or natural doubt, distrust, impatience, or the most subtle suggestions of the tempter, can move his simple trust in his Father, or wring from Him one act of self-assertion, the enemy changes front and the assault comes from another quarter. "You may be right," the voices seem now to be saying; "you may not be deceived, or dreaming, when you claim to be the Son of God, sent to redeem this fair world, which is now spread out before you in all its glory. That may be your origin, and that your work. But, living as you have done till now in a remote corner of a despised province, you have no experience or knowledge of the methods or powers which sway men, and establish and maintain these kingdoms of the world, the glory of which you are beholding. These methods and powers have been in use in your Father's world, if it be his, ever since man has known good from evil. You have only to say the word, and you may use and control these methods and powers as you please. By their aid you may possibly 'see of the travail of your soul and be satisfied;' without them you will redeem nothing but perhaps a man here and there — without them you will postpone instead of hastening the coming of your Father's kingdom, to the sorrow and ruin of many generations, and will die a foiled and lonely man, crushed by the very forces you have refused to use for your Father's service. If they were wholly evil, wholly unfit for the fulfillment of any purpose of his, would He have left them in command of his world till this day? It is only through them that the world can be subdued. Your time is short, and you have already wasted much of it, standing shivering on the brink, and letting the years slip by in that cottage at Nazareth. The wisest of your ancestors acknowledged and used them, and spread his kingdom from the river to the Great Sea. Why should you reject them?"

This, very roughly and inadequately stated, is some shadow of the utmost part or skirt, as it were, of the trial-crisis, lasting forty days, through which Christ passed from his private to his public career. For forty days the struggle lasted before He could finally realize and accept his mission with all that it implied. At the end of that time He has fairly mastered and beaten down every doubt as to his call, every tempting suggestion to assert Himself, or to accept or use any aid in establishing his Father's kingdom which does not clearly bear his Father's stamp and seal on the face of it. In the strength of this victory He returns from the desert, to take up the burden which has been laid on Him, and to set up God's kingdom in the world by the methods which He has learned of God Himself — and by no other.

Thus in following the life of Christ up to this point, so far as we have any materials, we have found its main characteristic to be patience — a resolute waiting on God's mind. I have asked you to test in every way you can, whether this kind of patience does not constitute the highest ideal we can form of human conduct, is not in fact the noblest type of true manliness. Pursue the same method as to this isolated section of that life, the temptation, which I readily admit has much in it that we cannot understand. But take the story simply as you find it (which is the only honest method, unless you pass it by altogether, which would be cowardly) and see whether you can detect any weakness, any flaw, in the perfect manliness of Christ under the strain of which it speaks — whether He does not here also realize for us the most perfect type of manliness in times of solitary and critical trial. Spare no pains, suppress no doubt, only be honest with the story, and with your own consciences.

There is scarcely any life of first-rate importance to the world in which we do not find a crisis corresponding to this, but the nearest parallel must be sought amongst those men, the greatest of their kind, who have founded or recast one of the great religions of the world. Of these (if we except the greatest of all, Moses) Mohammed is the only one of whose call we know enough to speak. Whatever we may think of him and the religion he founded, we shall all probably admit that he was at any rate a man of the rarest courage. In his case, too, it is only at the end of long and solitary vigils in the desert that the vision comes which seals him for his work. The silver roll is unfolded before his eyes, and he who holds it bids him read therein the decrees of God, and tells him, "Thou art the prophet of God, and I his angel."

He is unmanned by the vision, and flies trembling to his wife, whose brave and loving counsel, and those of his friends and first disciples, scarcely keep him from despair and suicide.

I would not press the parallel further than to remark that Christ came out of the temptation with no human aid, having trod the wine-press alone, serene and resolute from that moment for the work to which God had called Him.

It remains to follow his life in action, and to scrutinize its special characteristics there. And again I would ask you to sift every step thoroughly for yourselves, and see whether it will not bear the supreme crucial test from first to last. Apply that test, therefore, without scruple or limitation in respect of this special quality of manliness, from which we started on our inquiry. I have admitted, and admit again, frankly and at once, that if the life will not stand the test throughout, in every separate action and detail, the Christian hypothesis breaks down. For we may make allowances for the noblest and bravest men, for

Moses and Elijah and St. Paul, for Socrates and Luther and Mohammed, and every other great prophet, but we can make none for the perfect Son of man and Son of God. His life must stand the test under all circumstances, and at every moment, or the ground breaks through under our feet, and God has not revealed Himself in man to men, or redeemed the world by the methods in which Christendom has believed for nineteen hundred years.

PART V.

CHRIST'S MINISTRY. ACT I.

> "This perfect man, by merit called my son,
> To earn salvation for the sons of men."
> MILTON, *Paradise Regained*, Book I.

IT will be necessary for our purpose to follow in outline the events of our Lord's ministry as a consecutive narrative. If I do so without calling your attention to the endless difficulties and questions which have been fairly raised as to the occurrence and sequence of many of those events, it is not because I wish to ignore them myself, or to lead you away from the examination of them. In our time, which is, perhaps, before all things an age of criticism, much has been done towards the creation of a science of history, and therefore of a science of religion, which is the highest part of history. We have discovered, or at any rate have done much to perfect, the use of new and searching methods of investigation, and have applied, and are applying, these to every department of human knowledge and human life.

It was not to be expected, or indeed to be wished, that the new criticism should pause before that history, or the books containing it, which our forefathers held too sacred to be looked upon or treated as ordinary history. It has not paused, and, while respecting our fathers' reverent feeling for the books which have done so much for our nation and for the world, we may rejoice that it has not; and that friend and foe in this generation have been alike busy in turning all the light which recent research has placed within their reach upon the story of our Lord's ministry, and the gospel narratives in which it is contained.

We English were in danger of idolatry in this matter, — of putting the Book in the place of Him of whom it testifies, — and it is well for us that we have been shaken;

however roughly, out of a habit which fostered unreality in the very centre of our lives. We were inclined to claim for Christ's religion, and for its evidences, immunities which neither He nor his apostles ever claimed. That position has been abandoned, and the best representatives of every school of religious thought amongst us (so far as I am aware) now challenge the freest inquiry, and lend their own aid in carrying it on. And amongst the first, and not least formidable, difficulties which have met Christian writers has been that of harmonizing the writings of the four evangelists so as to make the several narratives fit into one continuous whole.

Whether it is possible that this can ever be done completely, in the absence of the discovery of new evidence, which there is no reason to look for, seems to be very doubtful. At any rate it has not been accomplished hitherto. But the general outline comes out clearly enough, and this is all we need in order to pursue our own particular inquiry satisfactorily.

Turning, then, to the point at which we have arrived, we shall find ourselves at once met by questions of detail as to our Lord's return from the wilderness after his temptation. Whether He returned to the scene of John's baptism, on the Jordan, and remained there for some days, or went straight back into Galilee from the desert; whether He commenced his active ministry at once, or even yet postponed it until John had been put in prison — are questions about which there is as yet no general concurrence of opinion.

You may each of you judge for yourselves of the difficulties by comparing the passages in the four gospels which relate to this period.

Taking this warning with us, we need trouble no further about the harmonies. Indeed, for our purpose, they are of very little consequence, for, take the narrative how we will, it divides itself beyond all question into several distinct and clearly marked periods. The first of these is that between the temptation and the formal opening of Christ's ministry in Galilee, marked by his first great discourse at Nazareth, the abandonment of his home, and the selection of the five first Apostles for special and continuous service. This first period extends at most over a few months, or more probably weeks, beginning a few days before the feast of the Passover, and ending in the early summer; at the time, not (so far as I am aware) exactly ascertained, when Herod Antipas seized John the Baptist and put him in prison. We must run through it shortly, noting the principal events, and then applying our test to such of them as seem to come within the scope of our inquiry.

The temptation over, Christ appears to have returned by Bethabara on his way to his Galilean home. The crowds were still pressing to John's baptism, and a group of the most earnest amongst them had already gathered round the Baptist, and were attaching themselves to his person, as the sons of the prophets round Elisha, the Apostles round Christ Himself, the companions of Medina round Mohammed.

To two of these disciples John points out Christ as that Son of God, of whom he was sent to bear record. They follow Him, spend a few hours of the afternoon with Him, and recognize Him as the Messiah. One of them, Andrew, brings his brother Simon Peter to Christ. He Himself calls Philip, who in his turn brings his friend Nathanael. With these five Christ starts for his home in Galilee.

These earliest followers, we may note, are almost certainly of the twelve Apostles, As to Andrew, Simon Peter, and Philip, who are expressly named, there is no question; and there is good reason to believe that the companion of Andrew, whose name is not given, was John, the son of Zebedee, and that Nathanael was the Apostle Bartholomew, whose name is constantly coupled in the gospels with that of Philip. Nathanael was of Cana of Galilee, of what trade we do not know; the other four were of Bethsaida, a suburb of Capernaum, fishermen on the Sea of Galilee.

They accompany Christ to Cana, Nathanael's home, where they meet Christ's mother, and are present at the marriage feast, at which his first miracle is wrought. From thence they follow him to Capernaum, and some of them go on with Him to Jerusalem to the Passover, at which He drives out the cattle-dealers from the outer court of the temple, and overthrows the tables of the money-changers.

This act fixes the attention of all Jerusalem upon Him, and brings Him at once under the notice of the Sanhedrim. One of its members, a Pharisee, seeks an interview with Him by night. He commits Himself neither to the mob nor to the nobleman. After the feast He remains for some time in the northern part of Judæa, where his fame attracts followers, whom his disciples baptize. He then passes through Samaria, still attended by his followers, stopping some days in the city of that name, and preaching there. They then go into Galilee, and, while the disciples apparently separate for the time to their own homes and pursuits, He returns to Nazareth, to begin his formal ministry amongst those who had known Him from his childhood. They turn upon Him in the middle of his first discourse, and attempt to murder Him. He leaves his old home for the neighboring village of Cana, where He is found by the ruler whose son is sick at Capernaum. He heals the child, and follows the father to that city, where He hears of the imprisonment of the Baptist, and at once enters on the second stage of his public career.

And now, following the narrative step by step so far, see if you can find any trace in it of a failure of courage, even for a moment. In the first place you will find, generally, that there is no wavering or hesitation at any point. The time for these is past, and, the call once recognized and accepted there is no shrinking or looking round, or going back. The strain and burden of a great message of deliverance to men has again and again found the weak places in the faith and courage of the most devoted and heroic of those to whom it has been entrusted. Moses pleads under its pressure that another may be sent in his place, asking despairingly, "Why hast Thou sent me?" Elijah prays for death. Mohammed passes years of despondency and hesitation under the sneers of those who scoff, "There goeth the son of Abdallah, who hath his converse with God!" Such shrinkings and doubtings enlist our sympathy, make us feel the tie of a common humanity which binds us to such men. But no one, I suppose, will maintain that perfect manliness would not suppress, at any rate, the open expression of any such feelings. The man who has to lead a great revolution should keep all misgivings to himself, and the weight of them so kept must often prove the sorest part of his burden.

But let us pass on to the particular events of this period. As to many of them the question of whether they are courageous or not, perhaps does not arise, except in so far as it arises on every act in our lives, each of which may, and indeed must, be done either manfully with perfect directness, or unmanfully with more or less adroitness. The man whose yea is yea and his nay nay, is, we all confess, the most courageous, whether or no he may be the most successful in daily life. And He who gave the precept has left us the most perfect example of how to live up to it. And this quality you will find shines out at once in these early conversations with Nathanael, Nicodemus, and the woman of Samaria, as much as in the discourses of his later years.

Before considering them we may glance at the purification of the temple, an act which at any rate should satisfy those who think courage best proved by physical daring. At this time, we must remember, He had no following, such as the crowd that swept after him on Palm Sunday, three years later, into the temple courts. But, leaving the act to speak for itself, look at the rare courage of the speech by which that act is justified when it is challenged. He, not even a Levite, a mere peasant from a despised province, had presumed to exercise authority in the very temple precincts! Jerusalem was full of worse idolatries, but the idolatry of the temple buildings was, perhaps, the strongest. The Jews seem to have regarded them as Christians have sometimes regarded the visible Church, or the Bible — as an object of worship; to have thought that if they perished God Himself would perish. And so Christ's answer goes straight to the root of their idolatry. His words were not understood by the crowd, or even by his own disciples, in their full meaning — that his body, and the body of every man, is the true temple of God. But they understood enough of them to see that He had no superstition about these splendid buildings of theirs, and was trying to lift them above local and national prejudices, and those who would not be lifted brooded over them till their day of vengeance came.

But there were those on whom the daring acts and words of Christ were already taking hold. Many of those who had come up to the Passover believed in Him, some even amongst the rulers. One of these we hear more of at once.

Nicodemus, we must remember, was a leading member of the Sanhedrim, a representative of that section of the rulers who, like the rest of the nation, were expecting a deliverer, a king who should prevail against the Cæsar. They had sent to the Baptist, and had heard of his testimony to this young Galilean, who had now come to Jerusalem, and was showing signs of a power which they could not but acknowledge. For, had He not cleansed the temple, which they had never been able to do, but, notwithstanding their pretended reverence for it, had allowed to be turned into a shambles and an exchange? They saw that a part of the people were ready to gather to Him, but that He had refused to commit Himself to them. This, then, the best of them must have felt, was no mere leader of a low, fierce, popular party or faction. Nicodemus at any rate was evidently inclined to doubt whether He might not prove to be the king they were looking for, as the Baptist had declared. The doubt must be solved, and he would see for himself.

And so he comes to Christ, and hears directly from Him, that He has indeed come to set up a kingdom, but that it is no visible kingdom like the Cæsar's, but a kingdom over men's spirits, one which rulers as well as peasants must become new men before they can enter — that a light has come into the world, and "he that doeth truth cometh to that light."

From beginning to end there is no word to catch this ruler, or those he represented; no balancing of phrases or playing with plausible religious shibboleths, with which

Nicodemus would be familiar, and which might please, and, perchance, reconcile, this well-disposed ruler, and the powerful persons he represented. There is, depend upon it, no severer test of manliness than our behavior to powerful persons, whose aid would advance the cause we have at heart. We know from the later records that the interview of that night, and the strange words he had heard at it, made a deep impression on this ruler. His manliness, however, breaks down for the present. He shrinks back and disappears, leaving the strange young peasant to go on his way.

The same splendid directness and incisiveness characterize his teaching at Samaria. There, again, He attacks at once the most cherished local traditions, showing that the place of worship matters nothing, the object of worship everything. That object is a Father of men's spirits, who wills that all men shall know and worship Him, but who can only be worshipped in spirit and in truth. He, the peasant who is talking to them, is Himself the Messiah, who has come from this Father of them and Him, to give them this spirit of truth in their own hearts.

The Jews at Jerusalem had been clamoring round Him for signs of his claim to speak such words, and in the next few days his own people would be crying out for his blood when they heard them. These Samaritans make no such demand, but hear and recognize the message and the messenger. The seed is sown, and He passes on, never to return and garner the harvest; deliberately preferring the hard, priest-ridden lake cities of the Jews as the centre of his ministry. He will leave ripe fields for others to reap. This decision, interpret it as we will, is that of no soft or timid reformer. Take this test again and compare Christ's choice of his first field for work with that of any other great leader of men.

This first period fitly closes with the scene at Nazareth. Here He returns, while the reports of his doings at the feast at Jerusalem are fresh in the minds of his family and fellow-townsmen. They are excited and divided as to Him and his doings. A thousand reasons would occur for speaking soft things, at such a moment, for accommodating His teaching, here at any rate, to the wants and tastes of his hearers, so as to keep a safe and friendly asylum at Nazareth, amongst the scenes and people He had loved from childhood. It is clear that some of his family, if not his mother herself, were already seriously alarmed and displeased. They disliked what they had heard of His teaching at Jerusalem and on His way home, which they felt must bring Him to ruin, in which they might be involved. He must have seen and conversed with them in his own home before that scene in the synagogue, and have had then to endure the bitter pain of alienating those whom He loved and respected, and had reason to love and respect, but who could not for the time rise out of the conventional, respectable way of looking at things.

To stand by what our conscience witnesses for as truth, through evil and good report, even against all opposition of those we love, and of those whose judgment we look up to and should ordinarily prefer to follow ; to cut ourselves deliberately off from their love and sympathy and respect, is surely, I repeat, one of the most severe trials to which we can be put. A man has need to feel at such times that the Spirit of the Lord is upon him in some measure, as it was upon Christ when He rose in the synagogue of Nazareth and, selecting the passage of Isaiah which speaks most directly of the Messiah, claimed that title for Himself, and told them that to-day this prophecy was fulfilled in Him.

The fierce, hard, Jewish spirit is at once roused to fury. They would kill Him then and there, and so settle his claims, once for all. He passes through them, and away from the quiet home where He had been brought up — alone, it would seem, so far as man could make Him so, and homeless for the remainder of his life. Yet not alone, for his Father is with Him; nor homeless, for He has the only home of which man can be sure, the home of his own heart shared with the Spirit of God.

PART VI.

CHRIST'S MINISTRY. ACT II.

> "What is it that ye came to note?
> A young man preaching from a boat."
> — A. CLOUGH.

THE second period of our Lord's ministry is one, in the main, of joyful progress and triumph, in which the test of true manliness must be more subtle than when the surroundings are hostile. It consists, I think, at such times in the careful watchfulness not to give wrong impressions, not to mislead those who are touched by enthusiasm, conscious of new life, grateful to Him who has kindled that life in them.

It is then that the temptation to be all things to all men in a wrong sense — to adapt and accommodate teaching and life to a lower standard in order to maintain a hold upon the masses of average men and women who have been moved by the words of lips touched by fire from the altar of God, — has generally proved too much for the best and strongest of the world's great reformers. It is scarcely necessary to labor this point, which would, I think, be sorrowfully admitted by those who have studied most lovingly and carefully the lives of such men, for instance, as Savonarola or Wesley. If you will refer to a recent and valuable work on the life of a greater than either of these, Mr. Bosworth Smith's "Mohammed and Mohammedanism," you will find there perhaps the best illustration which I can give you of this sad experience.

When Mohammed returns from Medina, sweeping at last all enemies out of his path, as the prophet of a new faith, and the leader of an awakened and repentant people, his biographer pauses to notice the lowering of the standard, both in his life and teaching. Power, he pleads, brings with it new temptations and new failures. The more thoroughly a man is carried away by his inspiration, and convinced of the truth and goodness of his cause and his message, the more likely is he to forget the means in the end, and to allow the end to justify whatever means seem to lead to its triumph. He must maintain as he can, and by any means, his power over the motley mass of followers that his mission has gathered round him, and will be apt to aim rather at what will hold them than at what will satisfy the highest promptings of his own conscience.

We may allow the plea in such cases, though with sorrow and humiliation. But the more minutely we examine the life of Christ the more we shall feel that here, again, there is no place for it. We shall be impressed with the entire absence of any such bending to expediency, or forgetting the means in the end. He never for one moment accommodates his life or teaching to any standard but the highest: never lowers or relaxes that standard by a shade or a hair's-breadth, to make the road easy to rich or powerful questioners, or to uphold the spirit of his poorer followers when they are startled and uneasy, as they begin halfblindly to recognize what spirit they are of. This unbending truthfulness is, then, what we have chiefly to look for in this period of triumphant progress and success, questioning each act and word in turn whether there is any swerving in it from the highest ideal.

It is not easy to mark off distinctly the time over which it extends, but it seems to me to commence with his return to Capernaum, after the healing of the centurion's son, when He hears of the imprisonment of John, and to end with the estrangement of many of his followers at his teaching as to the bread of life, and the nearly contemporaneous and final and open rupture with, and defiance of, the chief priests and scribes and Pharisees, when they change from suspicious and watchful critics into open and avowed enemies, baffled for the moment, but dogging his footsteps and thirsting for his blood.

It is upon his relations with these scribes and Pharisees more particularly that we must keep our attention fixed, as it is here, if anywhere, that we may look for a failure of nerve and truthfulness, and therefore of manliness.

We must gather our connected view of this period from all the narratives, and shall find the beginning most clearly indicated in St. Matthew, in the last part of the fourth chapter, where He recalls to his side Peter and Andrew and the sons of Zebedee — who appear to have left Him for the moment and to have returned to their boats and nets at Bethsaida — and opens his ministry in the lake cities by the Sermon on the Mount. For the end we must go to the eleventh chapter of St. Luke, where, in the house of a Pharisee, He speaks the words which madden Pharisees and lawyers into urging Him vehemently to speak of many things, and watching for the words which will enable them to entangle, and, as they think, to destroy Him.

First, then, as to the main facts so far as they are necessary for our purposes. We may note that our Lord accepts at once the imprisonment of the Baptist as the final summons to Himself. Gathering, therefore, a few of John's disciples round him, and welcoming the restless inquiring crowds who had been roused by the voice crying in the wilderness, He stands forward at once to proclaim and explain the nature of that new kingdom of God, which has now to be set up in the world. Standing forth alone, on the open hill-side, the young Galilean peasant gives forth the great proclamation, which by one effort lifted mankind on to that new and higher ground on which it has been painfully struggling ever since, but on the whole with sure though slow success, to plant itself and maintain sure foothold.

In all history there is no parallel to it. It stands there, a miracle or sign of God's reign in this world, far more wonderful than any of Christ's miracles of healing.

Unbelievers have been sneering at and ridiculing it, and Christian doctors paring and explaining it away ever since. But there it stands, as strong and fresh as ever, the calm declaration and witness of what mankind is intended by God to become on this earth of his.

As a question of courageous utterance (with which we are here mainly concerned), I would only ask you to read it through once more, bearing in mind who the preacher was — a peasant, already repudiated by his own neighbors and kinsfolk, and suspected by the national rulers and teachers; and who were the hearers — a motley crowd of Jewish peasants and fishermen, Romish legionaries, traders from Damascus, Tyre, and Sidon, and the distant isles of Greece, with a large sprinkling of publicans, scribes, Pharisees, and lawyers.

The immediate result of the sermon was to bow the hearts of this crowd for the time, so that He was able to choose followers from amongst them, much as He would.

He takes fishermen and peasants, selecting only two at most from any rank above the lowest, and one of these from a class more hated and despised by the Jews than the poorest peasant, the publicans. It is plain that He might at first have called apostles from amongst the upper classes had He desired it — as a teacher with any want of courage would surely have done. But the only scribe who offers himself is rejected.

The calling of the Apostles is followed by a succession of discourses and miracles, which move the people more and more, until, after that of the loaves, the popular enthusiasm rises to the point it had so often reached in the case of other preachers and leaders of this strange people. They are ready to take him by force and make him a king.

The Apostles apparently encourage this enthusiasm, for which He constrains them into a ship, and sends them away before Him. After rejoining them and rebuking their want of understanding and faith, He returns with them to the multitudes, and at once speaks of Himself as the bread from heaven, in the discourse which offends many of his disciples, who from this time go back and walk no more with him. The brief season of triumphant progress is drawing to an end, during which He could rejoice in spirit in contemplating the human harvest which He and his disciples seem to be already successfully garnering.

But, even while the prospect was fairest, while the people were surging round Him in the first enthusiasm of their new faith, there had been ominous signs of that antagonism of the rulers which was to end on Calvary, and we have now to glance at the relations of Christ with them during this same period.

This antagonism was of gradual growth. In the first instance many of the scribes and Pharisees seem to have followed Him, more for the purpose of hearing and watching, than in a spirit of direct hostility. In the Sermon on the Mount He only once alludes to them directly, when He tells his hearers that unless their righteousness exceeds that of the scribes and Pharisees there can be no place for them in this kingdom of which He is now proclaiming the laws. It does not appear, however, at first that they were alienated by what was then said, for soon afterwards we find Pharisees and doctors of the law from Jerusalem "and every town of Galilee and Judæa" sitting by while He teaches, "and the power of the Lord was present to heal them."

Now, however, they are aroused and startled by Christ's address to the palsied man — "Thy sins are forgiven thee." The cure of the man silences them for the moment. They are filled with fear, and glorify God, saying, "We have seen strange things to-day." But Christ's next act again rouses their jealousy afresh. He has not called any of them to his side; that, probably, they would have deemed presumption. They are waiting and watching; thinking, doubtless, that their presence gives a sanction and respectability to the young teacher, which He, and the crowds who come to hear and be healed, will in due course learn to appreciate. Meantime it might restrain Him and them from rash acts and words, which would ruin a national movement that might possibly be hereafter guided to the advantage of Israel.

But now, while the great men are thus balancing, and probably admiring themselves for their liberality, Christ singles out Levi the publican, calls him as an Apostle, and goes to his house to feast with a large company of other publicans. The great people remonstrate angrily. Such an act outrages all their notions of the orthodox conduct of a prophet. Christ replies, simply, that He has come to call sinners, not the righteous, to repentance.

A few days later an even more serious question is raised between them. On a Sabbath day his disciples pluck and eat the corn, and Christ justifies them. On the next Sabbath, while they are watching Him, He heals a man, with the obvious purpose of trying them, and claims to be Lord of the Sabbath as He had claimed power to forgive sins. They begin to be filled with madness, and commune what they can do to Him.

Still, however, the breach is not final. They have not abandoned the hope of using the young preacher and prophet for their purposes. So Simon, one of their number, invites Him to his house, and, though neglecting the usual courtesies of an entertainer (as out of place in the case of a peasant), is evidently not treacherous in the invitation. He might well flatter himself on his freedom from class prejudices, and feel that such condescension would have a good effect on his guest, and might lead Him in good time to rely on and consult persons moving in the upper ranks of Jewish society as to his future course.

The story of the woman, a sinner, who

gets into the room and anoints Christ's feet, and the use which He makes of the incident — to bring home to Simon's mind, with the most exquisite temper and courtesy, but with the most faithful firmness, his shortcomings as a host, and his want of true insight as a man — are amongst the finest illustrations we have of his method with the great and powerful of his nation. Before leaving the house He once more reasserts his power to forgive sins.

We must now follow Him to Jerusalem, to which He goes up to one of the feasts, and, at the headquarters of the scribes and Pharisees, deliberately raises afresh the burning questions which He had left rankling in the minds of the provincial hierarchy. He heals the impotent man at the pool of Bethesda on the Sabbath day, and sends him through the streets carrying his bed. Challenged to defend Himself (probably before the Sanhedrim), He claims, more explicitly than ever before, that God is his Father, and has given Him not only power to do mighty works, but "authority to execute judgment;" that their own Scriptures testify of Him as He who can give them life if they will come to Him for it. Upon which they, naturally enough, seek to slay Him; but He gets back unscathed to Galilee, and then follows the scene which I have referred to as the end of this period of his ministry.

The Pharisees are now dogging his footsteps wherever He goes, but even yet have not given up the hope of coming to some terms with One whom they cannot help acknowledging to wield a power over the people which has slipped away from themselves. Influenced possibly, by a discourse in which He upbraids the people as an evil generation, without specially alluding, as was so often his custom, to the people's leaders and teachers as those upon whom the chief guilt rested, they again invite Him into their own circle. But now the time is past for the kindly courtesy of the feast in Simon's house. The usual means of washing before meat are there, but He rejects them. They express a well-bred astonishment, and then follows that scathing denunciation of their hypocrisies and tyrannies, of their "inward parts full of ravening wickedness," which makes the breach final and irrevocable between the Son of Man and the rulers of Israel.

Thenceforth Christ has more and more to "tread the wine press alone," surrounded by bewildered followers, and powerful enemies resolved on his destruction, and unscrupulous as to the means by which it must be compassed.

PART VII.

CHRIST'S MINISTRY. ACT III.

> "By the light of burning martyr fires Christ's bleeding feet
> I track,
> Toiling up new Calvaries ever with the cross that turns
> not back." LOWELL.

WE have now reached the critical point, the third act in the world's greatest drama. All chance of the speedy triumph of the kingdom of God, humanly speaking, in this lake country of Galilee, — the battle-field chosen by Himself, where his mightiest works had been done and his mightiest words spoken, — the district from which his chosen companions came, and in which clamorous crowds had been ready to declare Him king, — is now over. The conviction that this is so, that He is a baffled leader, in hourly danger of his life, has forced itself on Christ. Before entering that battle-field, face to face with the tempter in the wilderness, He had deliberately rejected all aid from the powers and kingdoms of this world, and now, for the moment, the powers of this world have proved too strong for Him.

The rulers of that people — Pharisee, Sadducee, and Herodian, scribe and lawyer — were now marshaled against Him in one compact phalanx, throughout all the coasts of Galilee, as well as in Judæa.

His disciples, rough, most of them peasants, full of patriotism but with small power of insight or self-control, were melting away from a leader who, while He refused them active service under a patriot chief at open war with Cæsar and his legions, bewildered them by assuming titles and talking to them in language which they could not understand. They were longing for one who would rally them against the Roman oppressor, and give them a chance, at any rate, of winning their own land again, purged of the heathen and free from tribute. Such an one would be worth following to the death. But what could they make of this "Son of Man," who would prove his title to that name by giving his body and pouring out his blood for the life of man — of this "Son of God," who spoke of redeeming mankind and exalting mankind to God's right hand, instead of exalting the Jew to the head of mankind?

In the face of such a state of things to remain in Capernaum, or the neighboring towns and villages, would have been to court death, there, and at once. The truly courageous man, you may remind me, is not turned from his path by the fear of death, which is the supreme test and touchstone of his courage. True; — nor was Christ so turned, even for a moment.

Whatever may have been his hopes in the earlier part of his career, by this time He had no longer a thought that mankind could be redeemed without his own perfect and absolute sacrifice and humiliation. The cup would indeed have to be drunk to the dregs, but not here, nor now. This must be done at Jerusalem, the centre of the national life and the seat of the Roman government. It must be done during the Passover, the national commemoration of sacrifice and deliverance. And so He withdraws, with a handful of disciples, and even they still wayward, half-hearted, doubting, from the constant stress of a battle which has turned against Him. From this time He keeps away from the great centres of population, except when, on two occasions — at the Feast of Tabernacles and the Feast of the Dedication — He flashes for a day on Jerusalem, and then disappears again into some haunt of outlaws, or of wild beasts. This portion of his life comprises something less than the last twelve months, from the summer of the second year of his ministry till the eve of the last Passover, at Easter, in the third year.

In glancing at the main facts of this period, as we have done in the former ones, we have to note chiefly his intercourse with the twelve Apostles, and his preparation of them for the end of his own career and the beginning of theirs; his conduct at Jerusalem during those two autumnal and winter feasts; and the occasions when He again comes into collision with the rulers and Pharisees, both at these feasts and in the intervals between them.

The keynote of it, in spite of certain short and beautiful interludes, appears to me to be a sense of loneliness and oppression, caused by the feeling that He has work to do, and words to speak, which those for whom they are to be done and spoken, and whom they are, first of all men, to bless, will either misunderstand or abhor. Here is all the visible result of his labor, and of his travail, and the enemy is gathering strength every day.

This becomes clear, I think, at once, when, in the first days after his quitting the lake shores, He asks his disciples the question, "Whom do the world, and whom do ye, say that I am?" He is answered by Peter in the well-known burst of enthusiasm, that, though the people only look on Him as a prophet, such as Elijah or Jeremiah, his own chosen followers see in Him " the Christ, the Son of the living God."

It is this particular moment which He selects for telling them distinctly, that Christ will *not* triumph as they regard triumphing; that He will fall into the power of his enemies, and be humbled and slain by them. At once the proof comes of how little even the best of his own most intimate friends had caught the spirit of his teaching or of his kingdom. The announcement of his humiliation and death, which none but the most truthful and courageous of men would have made at such a moment, leaves them almost as much bewildered as the crowds in the lake cities had been a few days before.

Their hearts are faithful and simple, and upon them, as Peter has testified, the truth has flashed once for all, that there can be no other Saviour of men than this Man with whom they are living. Still, by what means and to what end the salvation shall come, they are scarcely less ignorant than the people who had been in vain seeking from Him a sign such as they desired. His own elect "understood not his saying, and it was hid from them, that they perceived it not." Rather, indeed, they go straight from that teaching to dispute amongst themselves who of them shall be the greatest in that kingdom which they understand so little. And so their Master has to begin again at the beginning of his teaching, and, placing a little child amongst them, to declare that not of such men as they deem themselves, but of such as this child, is the kingdom of heaven.

The episode of the Transfiguration follows; and immediately after it, as though purposely to warn even the three chosen friends who had been present against new delusions, He repeats again the teaching as to his death and humiliation. And He reiterates it whenever any exhibition of power or wisdom seems likely to encourage the frame of mind in the twelve generally which had lately brought the great rebuke on Peter. How slowly it did its work, even with the foremost disciples, there are but too many proofs.

Amongst his kinsfolk and the people generally, his mission, thanks to the cabals of the rulers and elders, had come by this time to be looked upon with deep distrust and impatience. "How long dost Thou make us to doubt? Go up to this coming feast, and there prove your title before those who know how to judge in such matters," is the querulous cry of the former as the Feast of Tabernacles approaches. He does not go up publicly with the caravan, which would have been at this time needlessly to incur danger, but, when the feast is half over, suddenly appears in the temple. There He again openly affronts the rulers by justifying his former acts, and teaching and proclaiming that He who has sent Him is true, and is their God.

It is evidently on account of this new

proof of daring that the people now again begin to rally round him. "Behold, He speaketh boldly. Do our rulers know that this is Christ?" is the talk which fills the air, and induces the scribes and Pharisees, for the first time, to attempt his arrest by their officers.

The officers return without Him, and their masters are, for the moment, powerless before the simple word of Him who, as their own servants testify, "speaks as never man spake." But if they cannot arrest and execute, they may entangle Him further, and prepare for their day, which is surely and swiftly coming. So they bring to Him the woman taken in adultery, and draw from Him the discourse in which He tells them that the truth will make them free — the truth which He has come to tell them, but which they will not hear, because they are of their father the devil. He ends with asserting his claim to the name which every Jew held sacred, "before Abraham was, I am." The narrative of the seventh and eighth chapters of St. John, which record these scenes at the Feast of Tabernacles, have, I believe, done more to make men courageous and truly manly, than all the stirring accounts of bold deeds which ever were written elsewhere.

The report of what had happened at the Feast of Tabernacles seems to have rekindled for a moment the fitful zeal of the people of Galilee. Christ does not, however, avail Himself of this reaction until the time comes for another return to Jerusalem to the Feast of Dedication, when, probably in the month of November or early in December, He returns once more to Capernaum, to prepare for his last journey. The Pharisees, impotent themselves for the moment, now hurry to warn Him that Herod is seeking to kill Him; but He passes on his way with perfect indifference.

The crowds seem, as of old, inclined to gather round Him again. He selects seventy from amongst them, and sends them on to prepare his route, following Himself, and, this time, it being his last pilgrimage, with the multitude.

And now, again, in the first days of this progress, the most trusted of the Apostles show how little, even yet, they understand their Lord, or their own work. When they see their Master once more at the head of a throng of followers the old spirit comes back on them as strongly as ever, and they are anxious to call down fire from heaven to consume those who will not receive Him. His rebuke and warning, yet again, pass by them, and get no hold on them. Rather, the incidents of the journey impress them more and more with the belief that, at last, the kingdom is coming with power. At length, at some point in the progress, they are amazed, and as they follow are afraid. Once more Christ takes them aside, and endeavors to dispel their dreams, repeating to them, in painful detail, what will happen to Himself at Jerusalem at the end of this journey; that He will be betrayed, delivered to the Gentiles, mocked, scourged, spat upon, crucified. In spite of this warning, and while it is yet ringing in their ears, we find James and John asking for the places of honor in the kingdom of their own imaginations!

At the feast He is met by the Pharisees and scribes in a somewhat different temper from that which they had shown at the end of his last visit. For He is once again at the head of a vast and eager multitude. They know that some, even of their own number, are inclined to believe in Him. They appeal to Him, passionately, to say who He is. He replies by referring to his former teaching about his Father, whom they claimed as their God, adding, "I and my Father are one."

Such a reply He well knew could only have one result. He was alone; and in the ears of those who surrounded Him He was speaking blasphemy, which could only be expiated by instant death. Yet He neither hesitates nor temporizes, but, when they seize stones to inflict the penalty, meets them with a bearing so calm and manly that they can no more cast the first stone at Him than they could three months before at the woman taken in adultery.

He leaves Jerusalem once more after the feast, going across Jordan with his Apostles to the country where John came preaching and baptizing, and remains there preaching to those who come to Him, until the news of Lazarus's death takes Him for a few days to Bethany. After the raising of his friend He returns to Peræa again, and leaves it only when the great caravan is passing by on its way to the Passover, in the early spring. He joins the caravan with his disciples, passing with it through Jericho, the city of priests, and selecting there the publican Zacchæus as his host, — a last lesson, by example, of the kind of material which will be used in building up his kingdom.

On the first day of the feast He rides into Jerusalem in apparent triumph, the city mob joining the pilgrim mob in greeting Him with loud Hosannas. Once more He cleanses the temple, and rouses the covetousness of the money-changers into active alliance with the bigotry of the priests, and the wild anger and jealousy of the rulers, to sweep this terrible Galilean revolutionist from the face of the earth, before He shall ruin them all.

For two days He continues to meet them in the temple and public resorts of the city, shaming, confuting, and denouncing them, and widening hour by hour that breach which was already gaping wide between the nation and city and their true Lord and King. The last scene in the temple, recorded in John, brings the long struggle to a close.

The more carefully you study this long wrestle with the blind leaders of a doomed nation, which has now come to an end, the more you will recognize the perfect truthfulness and therefore the perfect courage, which marks Christ's conduct of it. From beginning to end there is no word or act which can mislead friend or foe. The strife, though for life and death, has left no trace or stain on his nature. Fresh from the last and final conflict in the temple court, He can pause on the side of Olivet to weep over the city, the sight of which can still wring from Him the pathetic yearnings of a soul purified from all taint of bitterness.

It is this most tender and sensitive of the sons of men — with fibres answering to every touch and breath of human sympathy or human hate — who has borne with absolutely unshaken steadfastness the distrust and anger of kinsfolk, the ingratitude of converts, the blindness of disciples, the fitful and purblind worship, and hatred, and fear, of the nation of the Jews. So far, we can estimate to some extent the burden and the strain, and realize the strength and beauty of the spirit which could bear it all. Beyond and behind lie depths into which we can but glance. For in those last hours of his life on earth the question was to be decided whether we men have in deed and in truth a brotherhood, in a Son of Man, the head of humanity, who has united mankind to their Father, and can enable them to know Him.

PART VIII.

THE LAST ACT.

> " Thou seem'st both human and divine ;
> The highest, holiest manhood Thou ! "
> TENNYSON.

WE have reached the last stage, which is also the most critical one, of our inquiry. It is upon the accounts which we have of Christ's agony that the scornful denials of his manliness mainly rest. How, it is asked, can you Christians recognize as perfect man, as the head and representative of humanity, one who showed such signs of physical fear and weakness as Christ, by your own confession, showed in the garden of Gethsemane? Even without going to the roll of saints and martyrs, hundreds of men and women can be named who have looked a cruel death in the face without flinching, and endured tortures at least as painful as his with a constancy which was wanting in Him.

It was, indeed, a speech of this kind, in which the death of the Abolitionist leader, John Brown, was contrasted with that of Christ, as one so far superior in manliness that it ought to be enough of itself to shame Christians out of their superstition, which confirmed me in proposing this inquiry to you, as the most necessary and useful one we could engage in.

Now I freely admit that there is no recorded end of a life that I know of more entirely brave and manly than this one of Captain John Brown, of which we know every minutest detail, as it happened in the full glare of our modern life not twenty years ago. About that I think there would scarcely be disagreement anywhere. The very men who allowed him to lie in his bloody clothes till the day of his execution, and then hanged him, recognized this. "You are a game man, Captain Brown," the Southern sheriff said in the wagon.

"Yes," he answered, "I was so brought up. It was one of my mother's lessons. From infancy I have not suffered from physical fear. I have suffered a thousand times more from bashfulness;" and then he kissed a negro child in its mother's arms, and walked cheerfully on to the scaffold, thankful that he was "allowed to die for a cause, and not merely to pay the debt of nature, as all must."

There is no simpler or nobler record in the "Book of Martyrs," and in passing I would only remind you, that he at least was ready to acknowledge from whence came his strength. "Christ, the great Captain of liberty as well as of salvation," he wrote just before his death, "saw fit to take from me the sword of steel after I had carried it for a time. But He has put another in my hand, the sword of the Spirit, and I pray God to make me a faithful soldier wherever He may send me." And to a friend who left him with the words, "If you can be true to yourself to the end how glad we shall be," he answered, "I cannot say, but I do not think I shall deny my Lord and Master, Jesus Christ." The old Abolitionist would have been as amazed as any man at such a comparison as we are dealing with, and would have reminded us that, so far from treading the wine-press alone, he was upheld by the sympathy and enthusiasm of all of his own nation, and of the world outside his own nation, for whom he cared.

No such support had Christ. He knew too well that even the strongest of the little band which came with Him to the garden would deny Him before the light dawned over Olivet. And that sense of utter loneliness it was, more probably than all the rest of the burden which He was carrying, that wrung from Him the prayer of agony, recalled almost before it was uttered, that the cup might pass from Him, and caused the sweat as it were great drops of blood to fall from his brow as He knelt and prayed.

How the tradition of that agony and

bloody sweat has come to us is hard to say, as the nearest witnesses were asleep; but no Christian doubts that it is a true one, or that the passion of human weakness which then passed over his soul was a genuine shrinking from the unutterable anguish which was weighing it down to the dust.

But even admitting frankly all that is recorded of the agony and bloody sweat, such admission can only enhance the sublime courage of all that follows. It is his action when the danger comes, not when he is in solitary preparation for it, which marks the man of courage.

Let us just glance at this action. As Judas with his torchmen draws near He gathers Himself together, rouses his sleepy followers, and meets his enemy in the gate. There could have been no quailing in the glance before which the armed crowd of priests' retainers went backward and fell to the ground.

Follow Him through that long night: to the Sanhedrim chamber, where He Himself furnishes the evidence which the chief priest sought for in vain while He was silent — to the court of the palace, where He bore the ribaldry and dastard tortures and insults of the low Jewish crowd till morning, turning in the midst of them with the reminding look to Peter, which sent his last friend, broken down by the consciousness of his own cowardice, weeping into the night — to the judgment-seat of Pilate, and the scourgings of the Roman soldiers — to Herod's hall and the insults of the base Galilean court — back again to the judgment-seat of the representative of the divine Tiberius, and so to the final brutalities in the prætorium while the cross is preparing, and the blood which is dripping from the crown of thorns on his brow mingles with that which flows from the wounds of his scourgings — and find, if you can, one momentary sign of terror or of weakness.

In all the world's annals there is nothing which approaches, in the sublimity of its courage, that last conversation between the peasant prisoner, by this time a mass of filth and blood, and the Roman procurator, before Pilate led Him forth for the last time and pleaded scornfully with his nation for the life of their King. The canon from which we started must guide us to the end. There must be no flaw or spot on Christ's courage, any more than on his wisdom and tenderness and sympathy. And for the last time I repeat, the more unflinchingly we apply the test, the more clear and sure will the response come back to us.

We have been told recently, by more than one of those who profess to have weighed and measured Christianity and found it wanting, that religion must rest on reason, based on phenomena of this visible, tangible world in which we are living.

Be it so. There is no need for a Christian to object. He can meet this challenge as well as any other. We need never be careful about choosing our own battle-field. Looking, then, at that world as we see it, laboring heavily along in our own time

— as we hear of it through the records of the ages — I must repeat that there is no phenomenon in it comparable for a moment to this of Christ's life and work. The more we canvass and sift and weigh and balance the materials, the more clearly and grandly does his figure rise before us, as the true Head of humanity, the perfect Ideal, not only of wisdom and tenderness and love, but of courage also, because He was and is the simple Truth of God — the expression, at last, in flesh and blood, of what He who created us means each one of our race to be.

We have now finished our endeavor to look at the life of Christ from one point of view, and in special connection with one human quality. I trust it may prove to be only the first step for many of you in a study which will last your lives. At any rate it is one which the reverence which is felt by every member of this College for our founder ought to commend to us above all others.

He, as you all know, was never weary of impressing on us, term after term, year after year, that the aim of this place is to make good citizens, and that this can only be done by keeping vividly before ourselves, in all our work here, that common humanity which binds us all together by the ties of family, of neighborhood, of country. What that common humanity means and implies, he taught us, can only be understood by reference to a Son of Man, and Son of God, in whom we have all a common interest, through whom we have all a common spiritual relationship to his and our Father.

To bring this home to us all, as the central truth of our own lives, as the master-key of the confusions and perplexities in our own hearts and in the world around us, was the crowning work of his life, and I trust we have been true to his principle and his method in our attempt to realize the life of this Son of Man, and Son of God on this earth, which is so mysteriously at strife with the will of its Creator and Redeemer.

Into the heart of the mystery of that strife the wisest and best of us cannot penetrate, but the wayfaring man cannot help seeing that it is precisely around this life of the Son of Man and Son of God that the fiercest controversies of our time are raging. Is it not also becoming clearer every day that they will continue to rage more and more fiercely — that there can be no rest or peace possible for mankind — until all things are subdued to Him, and brought into harmony with his life?

It is to this work that all churches and sects, Catholic and Protestant, that all the leading nations of the world, known collectively as Christendom, are pledged: and the time for redeeming that pledge is running out rapidly, as the distress and perplexity, the threatening disruption and anarchy, of Christendom too clearly show. It is to this work too that you and I, every man and woman of us, are also called; and if we would go about it with any hope and courage, it can only be by keeping the life of Christ vividly before us day by day, and turning to it as to a fountain in the desert, as to the shadow of a great rock in a weary land.

From behind the shadow the still small voice — more awful than tempest or earthquake — more sure and persistent than day and night — is always sounding, full of hope and strength to the weariest of us all, "Be of good cheer, I have overcome the world."

Πορεύου καὶ σὺ ποίου ὁμοίως.

CONCLUSION.[1]

AN ADDRESS, DELIVERED AT CLIFTON COLLEGE, SUNDAY EVENING, OCTOBER, 1879.

> "They crowd upon us in this shade,
> The youth who own the coming years —
> Be never God or land betrayed
> By any son our Harvard rears."
>
> THE REV. R. LOWELL.

WHAT is it in such societies as yours that gives them so strong a hold on, so unique an attraction for, those who have been for years engaged in the rough work of life? That the fact is so I think no one will deny, explain it how they will. I at least cannot remember to have met with any man who will not own that a visit to one of our great schools moves and touches him on a side of his nature which for the most part lies quiet, almost dormant, but which he feels it is good for him should be stirred. He may go back to his work without an effort to explain to himself why these unwonted sensations have visited him, but not without a consciousness that he has had a change of air which has done him good

[1] Printed by request. — T. H.

— that he has been in a bracing atmosphere, like that at the top of some high mountain pass, where the morning sun strikes earlier and more brightly than in the valleys where his daily task must be done.

To him who cares to pursue the inquiry, I think the conviction will come, that to a stranger there is something at once inspiring and pathetic in such societies as this, standing apart as they do from, and yet so intimately connected with, the great outside world.

Inspiring, because he finds himself once again amongst these before whom the golden gates of active life are about to open, for good or evil — each one of whom holds in his hands the keys of those gates, the keys of light or of darkness, amongst whom faith is strong, hope bright, and ideals, untainted as yet by the world's slow stain, still count for a great power.

Pathetic, because he knows but too well how hard the path is to find, how steep to climb, on the further side of those golden gates — how often in the journey since he himself passed out from under them, his own faith and hope have burned dimly, and his ideal has faded away as he toiled on, or sat by the wayside, looking wistfully after it; till in the dust and jar, the heat and strain of the mighty highway, he has been again and again tempted to doubt whether it was indeed anything more than a phantom exhalation, which had taken shape in the glorious morning light, only to vanish when the workday sun had risen fairly above the horizon, and dispersed the colored mists.

He may well be pardoned if, at such times, the remembrance of the actual world in which he is living, and of the generation which moved into line on the great battle-field when he himself shouldered musket and knapsack, and passed into action out of the golden gates, should for a moment or two bring the pathetic side of the picture into strongest relief. "Where are they now who represented genius, valor, self-sacrifice, the invisible heavenly world to these? Are they dead? Has the high ideal died out of them? Will it be better with the new generation?"[1]

Such thoughts, such doubts, will force themselves at times on us all, to be met as best we may. Happy the man who is able, not at all times and in all places, but on the whole, to hold them resolutely at arm's length, and to follow

[1] Emerson.

straight on, though often wearily and painfully, in the tracks of the divine visitor who stood by his side in his youth, though sadly conscious of weary lengths of way, of gulfs and chasms, which since those days have come to stretch and yawn between him and his ideal — of the difference between the man God meant him to be — of the manhood he thought he saw so clearly in those early days — and the man he and the world have together managed to make of him.

I say, happy is that man. I had almost said that no other than he is happy in any true or noble sense, even in this hard materialist nineteenth century, when the faith, that the weak must to the wall, that the strong alone are to survive, prevails as it never did before — which on the surface seems specially to be organized for the destruction of ideals and the quenching of enthusiasms. I feel deeply the responsibility of making *any* assertion on so moot a point to such an audience in such a place as this; nevertheless, even in our materialist age, I must urge you all, as you would do good work in the world, to take your stand resolutely and once for all, at school and all your lives through, on the side of the idealists.

In doing so I trust and believe I shall not be running counter to the teaching you are accustomed to hear in this place. I know that I *should* be running counter to it if anything I may say were to give the least encouragement to dreaminess or dawdling. Let me say, then, at once and emphatically, that nothing can be farther from my wish or thought. The only idealism I plead for is not only compatible with sustained and vigorous work: it cannot be maintained without it.

The gospel of work is a true gospel though not the only one, or the highest, and has been preached in our day by great teachers. And I do not deny that the advice I have just been giving you may seem at first sight to conflict with the work-gospel. Listen, for instance, to the ring of it in the rugged and incisive words of one of our strongest poets: —

> " That low man seeks a little thing to do,
>   Sees it and does it.
> This high man, with a great thing to pursue,
>   Dies ere he knows it.
> That low man goes on adding one to one,
>   His hundreds soon hit.
> This high man aiming at a million,
>   Misses a unit."

This sounds like a deliberate attack on the idealist, a direct preference of low to high aims and standards, of the seen to the unseen. It is in reality only a wholesome warning against aiming at any ideal by wrong methods, though the use of the words " low " and " high " is no doubt likely to mislead. The true idealist has no quarrel with the lesson of these lines; indeed, he would be glad to see them written on one of the door-posts of every great school, if only they were ballasted on the other by George Herbert's quaint and deeper wisdom.

> " Pitch thy behavior low, thy projects high,
> So shalt thou humble and magnanimous be.
> Sink not in spirit : who aimeth at the sky,
> Shoots higher much than he that means a tree."

Both sayings are true, and worth carrying in your minds as part of their permanent furniture, and you will find that they will live there very peaceably side by side.

There is in truth no real antagonism between them. The seeming paradox, like so many others, disappears in the working world. In the stress of the great battle of life it will trouble no soldier who keeps a single eye in his head and a sound heart in his bosom. For he who has the clearest and intensest vision of what is at issue in that battle, and who quits himself in it most manfully, will be the first to acknowledge that for him there has been no approach to victory except by the faithful doing day by day of the work which lay at his own threshold.

On the other hand the universal experience of mankind — the dreary confession of those who have merely sought a "low thing," and "gone on adding one to one;" making that the aim and object of their lives — unite in warning us that on these lines no true victory can be had, either for the man himself or for the cause he was sent into the world to maintain.

No, there is no victory possible for boy or man without humility and magnanimity; and no humility or magnanimity possible without an ideal. I have been pleading with you boys to take sides with the idealists at once and through life. I have told you unless you do so you can neither be truly humble nor truly magnanimous. You may reply, "Well, that advice may be good or bad, we cannot tell, until you tell us *how* we are to side with them, and what you mean by an idealist." Such a reply would be only reasonable, and I will try to answer the demand it makes, or at any rate to give you a few hints which will enable you to work out the question for yourselves.

There is not one amongst you all, I care not how young he may be, who has not heard or felt the call in his own heart to put aside all evil habits, and to live a brave, simple, truthful life in this school. It may have come to you while listening in chapel or elsewhere to religious teaching, or in the play fields or dormitories; when you have been alone or in company, at work or at play, but that it has come, at some time, in some place, there is not a boy in this chapel who will deny. It is no modern, no Christian experience, this. The choice of Hercules, and numberless other Pagan stories, the witness of nearly all histories and all literatures, attest that it is an experience common to all our race. It is of it that the poet is thinking in those fine lines of Emerson which are written up in the Hall of Marlborough College:—

"So close is glory to our dust,
So near is God to man —

> When duty whispers low, 'thou must,'
> The youth replies, 'I can.'"

It does not wait for the reasoning powers to be developed, but comes right in upon the boy himself, appealing to him to listen and follow.

It is this whisper, this call, which is the ground of what I have, for want of a better name, been speaking of as idealism. Just in so far as the boy listens to and welcomes it he is becoming an idealist — one who is rising out of himself, and into direct contact and communion with spiritual influences, which even when he shrinks from them, and tries to put them aside, he feels and knows to be as real, and will live, I hope, to acknowledge to be more real than all influences coming to him from the outside world — one who is bent on bringing himself and the world into obedience to these spiritual influences. If he turns to meet the call and answers ever so feebly and hesitatingly, it becomes clearer and stronger. He will feel next, that just in so far as he is loyal to it he is becoming loyal to his brethren: that he must not only build his own life up in conformity with its teaching, must not only find or cut his own way straight to what is fair and true and noble, but must help on those who are around him and will come after him, and make the path easier and plainer for them also.

I have indicated in outline, in a few sentences, a process which takes a life-time to work out. You all know too, alas! even those who have already listened most earnestly to the voice, and followed most faithfully, how many influences there are about you and within you which stand across the first steps in the path, and bar your progress; which are forever dwarfing and distorting the ideal you are painfully struggling after, and appealing to the cowardice and laziness and impurity which are in every one of us, to thwart obedience to the call. But here, as elsewhere, it is the first step which costs, and tells. He who has once taken that, consciously and resolutely, has gained a vantage ground for all his life. That first step, remember, ought to be taken by English boys at our English schools.

And here let me turn aside for a moment to note for you what seems to me, looking from outside, the ideal for which you English boys should just now be specially striving. The strength and weakness of the nation of which you are a part will always be reflected powerfully in these miniature Englands, and there is a national weakness which is alarming all thoughtful Englishmen at this time. Our race on both sides of the Atlantic has, for generations, got and spent money faster than any other, and this spendthrift habit has had a baleful effect on English life. It has made it more and more feverish and unsatisfying. The standard of expenditure has been increasing by leaps and bounds, and demoralizing trade, society, every industry, and every profession until a false ideal has established itself, and the aim of life is too commonly to get, not to be, while men are valued more and more for what they have, not for what they are.

The reaction has, I trust, set in. A period of depression, such as not been known for half a century, has come, happily in time to show us how unreal and transitory is all such material prosperity, that a nation's life cannot stand any more than a man's in the things which it possesses. But the reign of Mammon will be hard to put down, and all wholesome influences which can be brought to bear upon that evil stronghold will be sorely needed.

Amongst these none should be more potent than that of our great schools. It is probably too late for the present generation of grown men to restore a sounder tone and set up a higher ideal. Those by whom it must be done, if it be done at all, are now growing up in such schools as this. There can be, I fear, no question that the outside world has been reflected in our schools. I hear on all sides stories of increased expenditure of all kinds. There must be fancy dresses for all games, and boys are made to feel uncomfortable who do not conform to the fashion, or who practice such useful and often necessary economies as wearing old clothes or traveling third-class. You know whether such things are true here. If they are, they are sapping true manliness, and tainting our national life at its roots. But the stain, I believe, has not sunk so deep, and the reaction may be swifter and deeper than elsewhere in societies bound together in so close an intimacy as must exist in such schools as this.

In no other portions of English society can public opinion be modified so swiftly and so radically as in a public school. One generation of brave boys may do it, and a school generation is only a short four or five years. I say, then, deliberately, that no man can gauge the value in English life at this present critical time of a steady stream of young men, flowing into all professions and all industries from our public schools, who have learnt resolutely to use those words so hard to speak in a society such as ours, "I can't afford;" who have been trained to have few wants and to serve these themselves, so that they may have always something to spare of power and of means to help others; who are "careless of the comfits and cushions of life," and content to leave them to the valets of all ranks. Many of us have hopes from all we hear and know of this and other such schools that such a stream of free and helpful young men may be looked for. Will you, boys, and, above all, you elder boys, who can give a tone to the standards and ideals of to-day here, which may last for many years, see that, so far at any rate as Clifton is concerned, such hopes shall not be disappointed?

And take my word for it, while you will be doing a great work for your country, and restoring an ideal which has all but faded out, you will be taking the surest road to all such success as becomes honest men to achieve, in whatever walk of life you may choose for yourselves. The outlook is by no means cheerful even for those who have learnt to live simply, and to estimate "comfits and cushions" at their true value, either in England or elsewhere. The following of false ideals has, I fear, thrown heavy odds for many years to come against the chances in our modern life of those who will not bow down to them.

It is more than thirty years since the wisest of American writers, and one of the best of American gentlemen, speaking to the young men of New England, made much the same sad confession as I am making to you to-day. "The young man," he says, "on entering life finds the way to lucrative employment blocked by abuses. The ways of trade are grown selfish to the borders of theft, and supple to the borders (if not beyond the borders) of fraud. The employments of commerce are not intrinsically unfit for a man, or less genial to his faculties; but these are now in their general course so vitiated by derelictions and abuses, at which all connive, that it requires more vigor and resources than can be expected of every young man to right himself in them. Has he genius and virtue? the less does he find them fit for him to grow in, and if he would thrive in them he must sacrifice all the brilliant dreams of boyhood and youth; he must forget the prayers of his childhood, and must take on him the harness of routine and obsequiousness. . . . I do not charge the merchant or manufacturer. The sins of our trade belong to no class, to no individual. One plucks, one distributes, one eats. Everybody partakes, everybody confesses — with cap and knee volunteers his confession, yet none feels himself accountable. He did not create the abuse, he cannot alter it. . . . It happens, therefore, that all such ingenuous souls as feel in themselves the irrepressible strivings of a noble aim, who by the law of their nature must act simply, find these ways of trade unfit for them, and they come forth from it. Such cases are becoming more common every day. But by coming out of trade you have not cleared yourselves — the trail of the serpent reaches into all the lucrative professions and practices of men. Each has its own wrongs. Each finds a very intelligent conscience a disqualification for success." And so further on he adds — " Considerations of this kind have turned the attention of many philanthropists and intelligent persons to the claims of manual labor as part of the education of every young man. If the accumulated wealth of the past generation is thus tainted — no matter how much of it is offered to us — we must begin to consider if it were not the nobler part to renounce it, and to put ourselves into primary relations with the soil and nature, and, abstaining from whatever is dishonest and unclean, to take each of us bravely his part with his own hands in the manual labor of the world."

It is a sad confession that our modern society has come to such a pass, but one which I fear holds as true for England as for America. That it will continue so no one who has faith in a righteous government of the world can believe. There seem to me signs on all sides that it is coming to an end, and that a new industrial world is already forming under the wreck of the old. But the time of change must be one of sore trial, and your generation will have to bear the strain of it. In such a time as this they only will be able to help their country in her need who have learned in early life the great lessons of simplicity and self-denial, and I don't hesitate to say that the worst education which teaches simplicity and self-denial is better than the best which teaches all else but this.

The first aim then for your time and your generation should be, to foster, each in yourselves, and each in your school, a simple and self-denying life — your ideal, to be a true and useful one, must have these two characteristics before all others. Of course purity, courage, truthfulness are as absolutely necessary as ever, without them there can be no ideal at all. But as each age and each country has its own special needs and weaknesses, so the best mind of its youth should be bent on serving where the need is sorest, and bringing strength to the weak places. There will be always crowds ready to fall in with the dapper, pliant ways which lead most readily to success in every community. Society has been said to be "always and everywhere in conspiracy against the true manhood of every one of its members;" and the saying, though bitter, contains a sad truth. So the faithful idealist will have to learn, without arrogance and with perfect good temper, to treat society as a child, and never to allow it to dictate. So treated, society will surely come round to those who have a high ideal before them, and therefore firm ground under their feet.

> "Coy Hebe flies from those that woo
> And shuns the hand would seize upon her;
> Live thou thy life, and she will sue,
> To pour for thee the cup of honor."

Let me say a word or two more on this business of success. Is it not, after all, the test of true and faithful work? Must it not be the touchstone of the humble and magnanimous, as well as of the self-asserting and ambitious? Undoubtedly; but here again we have to note that what passes with society for success, and is so labeled by public opinion, may well be, as often as not actually is, a bad kind of failure.

Public opinion in our day has, for instance, been jubilant over the success of those who have started in life penniless and have made large fortunes. Indeed, this particular class of self-made men is the one which we have been of late invited to honor. Before doing so, however, we shall have to ask with some care, and bearing in mind Emerson's warnings, by what methods the fortune has been made. The rapid accumulation of national wealth in England can scarcely be called a success by any one who studies the methods by which it has been made, and its effects on the national character. It may be otherwise with this or that millionaire, but each case must be judged on its own merits.

I remember hearing, years ago, of an old merchant who, on his death-bed, divided the results of long years of labor, some few hundreds in all, amongst his sons. "It is little enough, my boys," were almost his last words, "but there is n't a dirty shilling in the whole of it." He had been a successful man too, though not in the "self-made" sense. For his ideal had been, not to make money, but to keep clean hands. And he had been faithful to it.

In reading the stories of these last persons whom the English nation is invited to honor, I am generally struck with the predominance of the personal element. The key-note seems generally some resolve taken in early youth connected with their own temporal advancement.

This one will be Lord Mayor; this other Prime Minister; a third determines to own a fine estate near the place of his birth, a fourth to become head of the business in which he started as an errand-boy. They did indeed achieve their ends, were faithful to the idea they had set before themselves as boys; but I doubt if we can put them anywhere but in the lower school of idealists. For the predominant motive being self-assertion, their idealism seems never to have got past the personal stage, which at best is but a poor business as compared with the true thing. Try the case by a teste very one of you can apply directly and easily. One boy here resolves — I will win this scholarship; I will be head of the school; I will be captain of the eleven; and does it. Another resolves — this school shall be purer in tone, simpler in habits, braver and stronger in temper, for my presence here; does his best, but doubts after all whether he has succeeded. I need not say that the latter is the best idealist; but which is the most successful Clifton boy?

I must bring these remarks to an end, and yet have only been able to touch, and that very lightly, the fringe of a great subject. I am sure many of you have felt this; and I shall be surprised if some amongst you are not already listening to me with a shade of jealousy in your minds, which might formulate itself somehow, perhaps thus: "Is this talk about idealism quite straightforward? Have n't we heard all this before? — Self-denial, simplicity of life, courage, and the rest, are they not the first fruits of Christianity as we have been taught it? And we have been told, too, that this call of which you have been talking is the voice of Christ's spirit speaking to ours. Can any good come of swaddling these truths in other clothes which will scarcely fit them better, or make them more easy, or more acceptable?"

To which I am glad to reply from my heart — Truly; so it is. *Rem acu tetigesti.* Christ is, indeed, the great idealist. "Be ye perfect as your Father in heaven is perfect," is the ideal He sets before us — the only one which is permanent and all-sufficing. His own spirit communing with ours *is* that call which comes to every human being. But my object has been to get you to-night to look at the facts of your own experience — and, as I have said already, the youngest has *some* experience in these deep matters — without connecting them for the moment with any form of religion.

Supposing the whole Bible, every trace of Christendom, to disappear to-morrow, the same thing would, nevertheless, be occurring to you, and me, and every man. We should each of us still be conscious of a presence, which we are quite sure is not ourself, in the deepest recesses of our own heart, communing with us there and calling us to take up our twofold birthright as man — the mastery over visible things, and above all the mastery over our own bodies, actions, thoughts — and the power, always growing, of this mysterous communion with the invisible.

It is, therefore, that I have abstained from the use of religious phraseology, believing that, apart altogether from the Christian revelation, the idealist will, and must always remain, nearest to the invisible world, and therefore most powerful in this visible one.

I think this method is worth using now and then, because, no doubt, the popular verdict of this time is against idealism. If you have not already felt it, you will assuredly feel, as soon as you leave these walls, that your lot is cast in a world which longs for nothing so much as to succeed in shaking off all belief in anything which cannot be tested by the senses, and gauged and measured by the intellect, as the trappings of a worn-out superstition. Men have been trying, so runs the new gospel, to live by faith, and not by sight, ever since there is any record at all of their lives; and so they have had to manufacture for themselves the faiths they were to live by. What is called the life of the soul or spirit, and the life of the understanding, have been in conflict all this time, and the one has always been gaining on the other. Stronghold after stronghold has fallen till it is clear almost to demonstration that there will soon be no place left for that which was once deemed all-powerful. The spiritual life can no longer be led honestly. Man has no knowledge of the invisible upon which he can build. Let him own the truth and turn to that upon which he *can* build safely — the world of matter, his knowledge of which is always growing; and be content with the things he can see and taste and handle. Those who are telling you still in this time that your life can and ought to be lived in daily communion with the unseen — that so only you can loyally control the visible — are either willfully deceiving you, or are dreamers and visionaries.

So the high priests of the new gospel teach, and their teaching echoes through our literature, and colors the life of the streets and markets in a thousand ways; and a Mammon-ridden generation, longing to be rid of what they hope are only certain old and clumsy superstitions, — which they *try* to believe injurious to others, and are quite sure make them uneasy in their own efforts to eat, drink, and be merry, — applauds as openly as it dare, and hopes soon to see the millennium of the flesh-pots publicly declared and recognized.

Against which, wherever you may encounter them, that you young Englishmen may be ready and able to stand fast, is the hope and prayer of many anxious hearts; in a time, charged on every side with signs of the passing away of old things, such as have not been seen above the horizon in Christendom since Luther nailed his protest on the church door of a German village.

www.ingramcontent.com/pod-product-compliance
Lightning Source LLC
Chambersburg PA
CBHW030249170426
43202CB00009B/675